OUR COLONIES AND INDIA:

HOW WE GOT THEM, WHY WE KEEP THEM

CYRIL RANSOME

GYAN

Published by

Gyan Publishing House
5, Ansari Road
Daryaganj, New Delhi-110002
Phone: 011-47034999, 9811692060
E-mail: books@gyanbooks.com

Distribution Network
gyanbooks.com
India, USA, Canada, UK, Australia

ISBN: 978-93-7097-294-0 (PB)

First Published, 1885

2nd Impression 2025

Printed at: Gyan Press, Delhi.

OUR COLONIES AND INDIA:
HOW WE GOT THEM, WHY WE KEEP THEM

Author: CYRIL RANSOME

OUR COLONIES AND INDIA

Owing to the antiquity and rarity of this book, certain pages are regrettably absent, and readability is compromised due to the blurring of the original text. If you possess any insights regarding the availability of these missing sections, kindly inform us. Your assistance is crucial in ensuring the completion of this significant work for the benefit of future generations.

OUR COLONIES AND INDIA.

OUR COLONIES AND INDIA:

HOW WE GOT THEM,

AND

WHY WE KEEP THEM.

BY

CYRIL RANSOME, M.A. OXON.,

PROFESSOR OF MODERN LITERATURE AND HISTORY
IN THE YORKSHIRE COLLEGE, LEEDS.

"Every port over which the Union Jack floats is as free to all the world as to England."

CASSELL & COMPANY, LIMITED:

LONDON, PARIS, NEW YORK & MELBOURNE.

1885.

PREFACE.

THE following lectures were delivered in the spring of 1885, in the People's Hall of the Leeds Industrial Co-operative Society, before an audience composed almost entirely of working men. Their aim is to combat the impression which I fear is widely spread among the working classes—that they have little or no interest in our Colonies and Dependencies. For this purpose I have tried to give such an account of these as would place in a clear light the financial aspects of the case—a side of the question which naturally appeals strongly to those who are engaged in industry and commerce. At the same time, I have not neglected the moral side of our relations to our Colonies, and especially to the natives of India.

I have endeavoured as far as possible to suit my style to my audience; to avoid the use of technical terms or ill-defined political phrases; to confine myself to the prominent features of the subject; and to make my illustrations as simple as possible.

For statistics I have been mainly indebted to the "Statesman's Year-book for 1884;" "The Statistical Abstracts for the United Kingdom, and for the Colonial and other Possessions, from 1869 to 1883;"

"The Blue-book on East Indian Trade, March, 1885;" "The Report of the Select Committee on East Indian Railway Communication, 1884;" and Mr. H. S. Cunningham's "British India and its Rulers."

It has been impossible always to mention authorities, though I have done so in a few cases, where it seemed that controversy might arise. I wish, however, to express my obligation to Professor Seeley, whose "Expansion of England" has done so much to call attention to this important question. In the discussion of the *value* of the Colonies and India I have followed a course of my own; but it is simply impossible to lecture on the *history* of Greater Britain without constantly treading in Mr. Seeley's footsteps. I wish, therefore, to thank him; and hope that these Lectures may do something towards arousing an interest in the subject he has so much at heart, among those who have not yet had the good fortune to make the acquaintance of the "Expansion of England."

CONTENTS.

OUR COLONIES AND INDIA.

LECTURE I.

WHAT OUR COLONIES WERE, AND HOW WE GAINED THEM.

THERE is a story told of a certain English statesman, suddenly called upon to undertake the duties of Secretary of State for the Colonies, who said to his secretary, "Don't you think it would be a good thing to get down a map, and let us see where these places are?" I do not know whether this story is literally true, but I think it represents a truth, namely, that considering that we, the English people, are practically the rulers of two hundred and fifty millions of people in India, and indirectly have a great deal to do with the welfare of ten million Englishmen, settled in Colonies spread over the surface of the globe, we are probably more ignorant of the people and countries for whom we are responsible, than any rulers who have ever attempted the task of governing a great dominion.

Why this is, it is hardly needful to inquire. Perhaps it is the vastness of the subject; perhaps it is its dulness; more probably still it is due to our not sufficiently recognising the enormous responsibility which lies upon each one of us. But, believing as I do, that Colonial questions, and matters of foreign politics, arising out of Colonial and Indian questions, will be the subjects which will in the future engross a great part of the time and tax to the utmost the wisdom of Parliament, I think it is not merely our interest, but our duty, to study the history and conditions of our empire, and to try to learn, from the history of the past, any lessons which may be of service to us in the conduct of the future.

I propose to ask you to turn your attention in this lecture to that part of the question which relates to the acquisition of our Colonies, because to understand their history is the first step towards realising their present condition. To do this, it will be needful to go back somewhat far into the past. It is a proverb that "Rome was not built in a day," and therefore a great institution like the British Empire, larger than anything the Romans ever possessed, and comprising regions whose very existence was unknown to them, has its springs deep bedded in the past, and its development is part of the history, not of England only, or even of Europe, but of the world.

If you will turn your mind to the earliest civilised states of which we read in the Bible, such as Babylon and Egypt, you will remember that they were founded by nations who dwelt upon the banks of such rivers as the Euphrates and the Nile.

Countries like Egypt and Babylonia were prosperous, because their soil was rich and fertile, and because their river acted as a high road by which men could trade one with another. At a later time we find the most civilised nations were all living round the Mediterranean Sea. There were to be found Tyre, Greece, Rome, and Carthage, all of whom traded with each other and with Egypt, and by whom Colonies were established, along the shores of the Mediterranean, both in Europe, Asia, and Africa. These nations outstripped the ancient Egyptians and Babylonians in civilisation, because they had greater powers of development than nations which were cooped up along the banks of a single river; so that we see that civilisation made a great stride when it changed its home from the banks of a river to the shores of the sea. Rome was more military and less commercial than the other States, so that in time she conquered them, and brought the whole of the shores of the Mediterranean under her sway, and by conquering Britain, which had hitherto been outside the pale of civilisation, she did the Britons the great service of bringing them within its limits.

For centuries the Mediterranean remained the centre of civilisation. Though the Roman Empire was overrun on the one side by the Goths and Germans, and on the other by the Mohammedans, the European nations still looked to the Mediterranean. The only trade which was carried on outside the Mediterranean and the small, almost inland seas of the North of Europe was with India, and this was carried on by means of caravans, which brought Indian goods to the shores of the Mediterranean, whence they were brought by sea to the countries of their purchasers. Of India itself men knew very little. China had scarcely been heard of; and no one had penetrated into Africa further than to Abyssinia in the north, or to Morocco in the west. No one thought of any other lands, because for a long time they believed that the earth was flat, and, therefore, there was no reason why its boundaries should not be anywhere; and even when it was discovered to be round, it was thought to be much smaller than it really is; so that, after all, there seemed no reason why the lands which were known should not be sufficient to fill it.

However, at the end of the fifteenth century—that is about the time when Henry VII., the first of the Tudors, was reigning in England—men's whole view of geography was upset by two events: Christopher Columbus, sailing due west, discovered America; and Vasco de Gama, doubling the Cape of Good Hope, made his way to India. It is impossible to over-estimate the importance of these discoveries. They altered the whole basis of power. The Mediterranean was displaced from her ancient position as the centre of civilisation. Her place was taken by the Atlantic, and power came to be estimated, not by a nation's importance in Europe, but by its position in the world. The little Republics of Italy, such as Florence and Venice, ceased to be important, just as Babylon had done before them; and Spain, Portugal, France, and England, which stood on the Atlantic, as Greece and Carthage had stood on the Mediterranean, became the most powerful states in the world.

You will notice that neither the discovery of America, nor of the new road to India, was made by Englishmen. The honour of these fell to Spain and Portugal, and these two nations naturally claimed to do what they liked with their new discoveries. There was, however, some fear that they might quarrel between themselves; but this danger was removed by a very simple plan. You will hardly believe it, but the theory of those days was, that all islands and newly-discovered countries belonged to the Pope, and no one thought for a moment that pagans possessed any claim to the regions they happened to inhabit. When the Pope was asked to decide between the claims of the Spaniards and the Portuguese, he settled the matter thus. He held the orthodox view that the world was flat, and, taking a map, he drew a straight line west of the Azores, and gave all that lay west of the line to the Spaniards; all that lay east of it to the Portuguese. Of course the further each went the further they would be apart, so that the decision settled the difficulty for all time.

If the English had respected the decision of the Pope, they would have been shut out from all share in the New World; but, fortunately, shortly afterwards England threw off the papal authority, and one result of the Reformation was that we were able to make a push for a share in the markets which were being opened up. Now we must remember that it was the theory of all the European nations that Colonies should only be allowed to trade with the mother country, and the English saw that, if they did not bestir themselves, they would be shut out of the new markets, and lose the chance of development which Spain and Portugal had seized. Of course our ancestors might have sat down quietly at home, and said that "it was no use crying over spilt milk," or perhaps have submitted the matter to arbitration; but they did not. We were not on very good terms with Spain at the time, so our sailors fitted out ships, and paid themselves for being cut out from trading with the Spanish Colonies by seizing the Spanish treasure ships as they came home. These attacks on his trade made the Spanish King, Philip, furious, and had more to do with his sending the Spanish Armada than anything Queen Elizabeth did.

The defeat of the Armada ruined Philip's naval power, and the English and Dutch first plundered his vessels, and then began to found Colonies themselves in lands which Spain claimed. Moreover, about the same time Spain conquered Portugal, so that the Portuguese Colonies were open to the same attacks; and so England and Holland systematically set to work to enrich themselves at the expense of the first discoverers. They played the part of the eagle which takes from the buzzard the lamb which it has stolen from the shepherd. It was partly because his desire for alliance with Spain interfered with this that James I. was so unpopular in England.

The Colonies planted in the New World were of three kinds. The first idea of the discoverers was to find gold, and the first Colonies were planted for the purpose of working the gold mines. Such were the Spanish Colonies of Mexico and Peru. The next plan was to grow tropical plants, such as the sugar-cane, to supply the home market. These were cultivated on a large scale by planters, who employed first the labour of the natives, and then, when these were found too weak for the task, the labour of negroes imported specially from Africa. Of the second kind were the West Indian Islands. To these two classes belonged all the Spanish and Portuguese Colonies. There was plainly room for a third sort of Colony—namely, one in which the Colonists should settle and labour with their own hands, as they did at home, in the pursuit of agriculture. The Spanish and Portuguese had no Colonies of this type, but to it most of the English Colonies belonged.

At the beginning of the seventeenth century, England had made no permanent settlement in America, but shortly afterwards she secured the Bermudas, a group of islands situated in the Atlantic, off the coast of North America, which became the basis of her Colonial Empire. The Spanish and Portuguese Colonies had mostly been sent out by Government: the English Colonies were the work of private individuals. For several reasons, during the reigns of James I. and Charles I., Nonconformists and Roman

Catholics were ready to quit England, and these emigrants, with a few adventurous persons who belonged to the Established Church, founded in America a series of settlements, in which they thought they would be happier than they were at home. These Colonies differed from each other from the first: Virginia was aristocratic, Church of England, and slave-holding; Maryland was Roman Catholic and slave-holding; the New England States were Puritan and free.

These settlements were scattered along the eastern shores of the Atlantic. Between them lay New Amsterdam—now New York—owned by the Dutch, and south of them lay Florida, which was Spanish. Still further south lay the basin of the Mississippi; while to the north lay Acadie, which we now call Nova Scotia, and the basin of the St. Lawrence, which we now call Canada; these three last were in the hands of the French. Each of the English Colonies had its own little Parliament, but its governor was sent from England, and it was only allowed to trade with the mother country. Such were the beginnings of the colonisation of North America.

At the time, then, of Oliver Cromwell—that is, in the middle of the seventeenth century—the New World was shared between Spain, Portugal, France, Holland, and England. Of these Spain and Portugal had by far the largest share; then came France, with its large territories in North America; and, lastly, Holland and England. Holland had little in America, but had considerable settlements in the Spice Islands off the south-eastern coast of Asia, including the Isle of Java; while England had only her small settlements on the coast of North America and the Bermudas. Hitherto the nations had rivalled each other in a race who should seize territory occupied by natives only. Oliver Cromwell began a fight for the possession of the Colonies themselves. For some years the English fleet had been growing in power, and Cromwell declared war upon Spain, and sent his ships to seize Jamaica, which we then took from the Spaniards, and hold to the present day.

This was the beginning of a new period in European warfare. In every war, from that time to the Battle of Waterloo, England always made it her chief business to seize the Colonies of her rivals, and in this way to add to her Colonial possessions at the expense of her neighbours. Whether she had any moral right to do this or not is another question; but the fact that, up to 1815, most of our Colonies were obtained by taking them from other people, is without dispute, and it is better to face the fact at once.

The attempt to increase our Colonial possessions at the expense of other nations was coupled with an effort to get as much trade as possible into our own hands. At that time the Dutch did most of the carrying trade of Europe—that is, it was their practice to carry goods from the port of one nation to that of another, paying themselves by buying the goods at one place, and selling them at a dearer rate at another. In this way they had created a large mercantile marine, protected by a powerful navy. The English were very jealous of this business, and to destroy it, passed certain laws, called the Navigation Acts, and as these Acts regulated the trade between the mother country and the Colonies, they had very great importance. By them no goods might be brought to England except in English ships, or in ships belonging to the nation where the goods were made. These laws struck a fatal blow at Dutch commerce. They were naturally resented, and during the time of the Commonwealth, and of Charles II., the two nations were continually at war. The Dutch power, however, steadily declined, and so gave England two important additions to her Colonies, one the State of New Amsterdam—now New York—which formerly divided the New England Colonies from Virginia, the other St. Helena, off the south coast of Africa, which, before she took the Cape of Good Hope, was most useful as a house of call for our ships on their way to and from India. This struggle with the Dutch States relieved her of a very formidable rival, and by great good luck, owing to the accession of William of Orange to the English throne, she was able for some time to keep the Dutch on her side.

England was then able to turn her attention to her more dangerous rival, France. Now if you think of what our relations with France have been at different times, you will see they fall under four great periods. During the fourteenth and fifteenth centuries we were, as a rule, fighting the French. Those were the days of Cressy and Poitiers, of Agincourt and Joan of Arc. Then, in the sixteenth and seventeenth centuries, we were, as a rule, at peace with France; indeed, no fighting of importance took place between the English and French from the loss of Calais, in the reign of Mary, till the battles of the time of William III. Then began a series of wars which lasted from the accession of William III., with short intervals, till the Battle of Waterloo in 1815. This was followed by a period of peace, during which France was often closely allied with England, and fought on her side, as in the Russian war.

When we see, in reading history, that events can be classed under such large heads as these, we may be sure that there is some cause for them. And if we find two nations for long intervals at war, then for long periods at peace, it will not do to offer as an explanation for the wars the sole reason that "kings are ambitious," because there were kings all the time, who were as likely to be ambitious at one time as another.

I should like to point out another fact. If wars were caused solely by the ambition of kings, we should find most wars when kings had most power. But how do you account for the fact that the time of the Tudors and Stuarts, when the kings had great power, were on the whole peaceful, while the times of Edward III. and Henry V., and of George I. and George II., when Parliament had very great power, so great, in fact, that the kings could not make war for a moment unless they could get Parliament to grant them supplies, were both times of war?

Now I will offer the explanation which I believe

to be true. In the times of Cressy and Agincourt, Parliament readily voted money because they thought (1) that if the King of England became King of France, they would have less taxes to pay; (2) that there was a danger lest the French should conquer Belgium, which was then our best customer for English wool; and (3) that it was of great consequence to them to keep possession of Calais and Guienne (the country of which Bordeaux is the chief town), to which we sent wool in exchange for wine. So long as Parliament thought there was a chance of securing these objects, they voted money readily enough; but in time they became convinced that the permanent conquest of France was impossible, and they then gave up the struggle, because "the game was not worth the candle." It is, however, worth noticing that the kings became aware of this and wished for peace, while their subjects were still clamouring for war.

Then came the time of peace with France. This was due, not to kings being less ambitious, but to the fact that England had given up the dream of conquering France, that Belgium had passed into the hands of Spain, and that English merchants were engaged in opening markets in the New World. These attempts brought us into collision, not with France, but with Spain and Holland; and, therefore, wars with Spain and Holland take the place of wars with France.

We now come to the third set of wars: those which began with William of Orange, and ended with the

Battle of Waterloo. These wars were the great event of the eighteenth and beginning of the nineteenth centuries. During these 126 years, from 1689 to 1815, we were engaged in seven great wars, the longest of which lasted twelve years, the shortest seven. These wars either began as wars with France, or invariably soon became so. There must, therefore, have been some reason, apart from the ambition of kings, which forced the English continually to be fighting the French. Perhaps you will say that it was the ambition of the nobles and gentlemen. Facts answer that this was not the case. During a great part of this time, the landowners had not the chief power in directing the policy of the Government. Indeed they opposed the war, and the advocates of fighting were the Whigs, who rested for support on the merchants and middle classes. We are, therefore, led to suspect that these wars were mercantile wars, and this is the case. We were forced to fight by the strongest instinct of humanity—the instinct of self-preservation.

The great reasons of these struggles were these—(1) the English were afraid that the French would take from them the Colonies they had, and so close their markets; and (2) they saw in war the chance of enlarging their own markets at the expense of the French. If we want, therefore, to estimate the value of these wars, we must ask ourselves—(1) Was the danger of the loss of the English Colonies real? (2) Did we get any solid value by conquering French Colonies? If we succeeded in this we may put it down to the credit side of the account. On the other side, we must put down the sums paid in the war as well as the National Debt.

Now I believe that this is not the usual way in which our accounts are balanced. I have seen what professed to be national balance-sheets, which seemed to put National Debt on one side in very big black type, and glory on the other in very thin red type. I do not think we pay much compliment to the sense of our ancestors by doing their accounts for them in this way.

If we heard that a certain capitalist had been for years engaged in working a mine, that every year he had laid out large sums in the working, that from time to time he had borrowed capital which he had laid down in the business, that the mine was a very dangerous one, in which great risks had to be run, and that from time to time terrible accidents happened; and if you were told that all he had got out of it had been—glory, you would say at once that such a man was a lunatic, and ought to be put into an asylum at once. I do not believe that our great-grandfathers were so foolish as that, and I think I can show you that they were not.

I will now give another illustration. It is the case of a gentleman who rented from one of the Colonial Governments a large sheep run. It was a good run, and he made a big income from it. Presently a change was made in the laws of the country, and he and others were allowed to select as freeholds such lands as they chose up to a certain size. Of course he chose as much of his own farm as he could, but other selectors who had nothing to do with him picked out the pieces which they thought would do him the most harm. His farm was ruined by being broken up. He had a large family to provide for. What was he to do? I will tell you what he did. He borrowed money, and bought out the free selectors. The result was that for a time he was crippled by the weight of his debt; but he has the prospect of paying it off; and when he has done that, he will find a fine freehold estate, and be a far richer man than before.

Now this seems to be an exact illustration, on a small scale, of what we Englishmen have done on a large one. We, too, were afraid that our estate was going to be broken up; we, too, had a large family; and we spent money and borrowed money to keep the property together, and to extend it. From our point of view as a nation we have to set one side of our account against the other and see whether our transaction paid.

It is very often said that England has very little to show for her National Debt. Nothing to show for the National Debt! It is the price we pay for the largest Colonial Empire the world has ever seen.

Take, for example, the war in which Blenheim was the best known battle. This war was opposed by the landowners; it was supported by the mercantile classes. It added £23,408,235 to the National Debt, besides what was spent year by year. Apparently the matter in dispute was whether an Austrian Prince or a French Prince should sit on the throne of Spain;

in reality it was to prevent—(1) the restoration of the Stuarts; (2) the union of the Spanish and French Colonies against England. The war came to an end at the Treaty of Utrecht, 1713. The Whigs, who had promoted the war, loudly cried out that the terms were disgracefully bad. Let us see what we gained. (1) France was incapable for many years of helping the Jacobites. (2) The French and Spanish Colonies were not joined. (3) Our Colonies were quite safe. (4) We annexed what is now called Nova Scotia and New Brunswick, and secured Newfoundland. (5) We acquired Gibraltar and Minorca in the Mediterranean. (6) We gained a monopoly of the slave-trade, and the right to send one ship a year to trade with the Spanish Colonies.

Our next wars were wars with Spain, and grew out of the Spaniards' interference with our Colonists, and their attempt to prevent their own Colonies from trading with us; but I want to keep to great things, so I pass on to the Seven Years' War, which lasted from 1756 to 1763. The nominal cause of this war was an attack of the French and Austrians on Frederick of Prussia. England, however, thought it worth while to join, and we must see what she got by it.

When it began, the French owned in North America the country through which the chain of great lakes, which empty themselves into the St. Lawrence, flows, and also the valley of the Mississippi; they claimed besides the territory which lay between the two—that is to say, they blocked the English Colonies on the north, on the south, and towards the west, and they showed the greatest determination to keep the English Colonists to this little strip of sea-coast between the mountains and the Atlantic. The Colonists resented this, and they were constantly fighting the French, even when the mother countries were at peace. This led to the English joining the King of Prussia, and paying money to help him to fight the French. What did they hope to gain by this? Clearly, so long as the energies of the French were employed at home they could not help their Colonies abroad, and so the English got the chance of enriching themselves at their neighbour's expense. After a time Spain joined the war, so we got an opportunity of attacking her Colonies too.

This war was brought to a close by the peace of 1763. The peace was the act of George III. and his party, and again the nation cried out that they had not gained as good terms as they ought. In the war the English had almost stripped the French of their West Indian Islands, and these were returned at the Treaty. The trade with one of these alone—Martinique—during two years had been very valuable: the English had exported £300,000 worth of English goods—that is, we had found an additional market for £300,000 worth of goods, which we should not have been able to sell otherwise. This shows that the conquest of these islands was a direct pecuniary advantage to our ancestors, and they saw in it a very good reason for war. Now let us turn to the bill. It runs thus:—Added to the National Debt, in addition to sums spent each year, £52,219,912.

Gained (1) Canada; (2) Florida, the southern boundary of the English Colonies; (3) the opportunity for our Colonies to spread inland; (4) Grenada, St. Vincent, Dominica and Tobago, sugar islands in the West Indies.

We now come to a very inglorious page in our history, namely, that in which the folly of George III. lost us the Colonies which have since become the United States. As the history of this event, from the point of view of a warning, is well worth examining, the subject, though painful, must be discussed. What was the reason of it? In the first place the majority of the northern Colonies which had been founded in the time of Charles I. had never been closely attached to the mother country. As early as the time of Charles II. they had declared that they were only united to her by civility. What, however, had kept them close to us? The answer is, *fear of France.* Now our very success in the last war removed this fear. Wolfe's victory at Quebec shattered this tie to the mother country. The capture of Florida removed all fear of attack from Spain. Still there was no reason why the two countries should not remain bound by the tie of civility. What was it that broke this? (1) The enforcement of the rule that the Colonists should not trade with the Spanish Colonies. (2) The attempt of George III. and his friends to insist on the claim of Parliament to tax the Colonies. Expense had been incurred for the sake of the Colonies for which it was fair that they should pay; and the Colonists would have paid, but they claimed, like other Englishmen, to vote their own taxes, and not to have them levied by an arbitrary ruler, such as the British Parliament was to them. These were, I believe, the causes why we lost the American Colonies. Ignorance made us insist on these claims, in spite of the warning of the ablest men on both sides of the water; and the great moral we have to draw from it is *not to be so foolish again.*

The English made tremendous efforts to bring the Colonies to submission, but when the latter were aided by France and Spain, who smarted under their own losses, they could not do it, and only the victory of Rodney on the seas saved them from losing their West Indian Colonies as well. The debt was increased by £100,000,000, and they came out of the war in 1783, only holding Canada and Nova Scotia, and their West Indian Islands, a few places on the coast of Africa, and Gibraltar. I purposely leave India out of consideration for the present.

We next come to the wars of the French Revolution. Again we are liable to have our sight blinded by the events on the surface. We hear a great deal of Burke's attack on the Republicans; we do not pay sufficient regard to what we gained. In the war, England found herself in turn opposed to France, Spain, and Holland, the only nations on the Continent which had many Colonies. What is the great fact of the war? It is this. We went into it stripped of our Colonies. We came out of it with a new Colonial Empire, and a large dependency in Asia as well.

The first part of the war, which added to the debt £226,000,000, was closed by the Peace of Amiens in 1802. By that peace we kept Trinidad, ceded by Spain, and Ceylon, by the Dutch; during the war we gained Malta, which was never restored.

The second part of the war, carried on from 1804 to 1815, was not, like the first, an attack upon the French Republic, but a defensive war against Napoleon. That statesman never looked on England as a merely European power; he always regarded her as a world-wide empire; and his great aim was to ruin her as such by attacking India and our Colonial Empire. "This old Europe tires me," he said, and by saying so he meant that he had grasped the idea that States must now be measured, not by their size relative to Europe, but by their size relative to the world. Happily for us, Napoleon was foiled in these efforts by two causes—(1) the victories of Nelson, which gave England the command of the seas; (2) the way in which England, by subsidising the European States, raised up coalition after coalition to employ Napoleon in wearing out his strength against the Continental powers. This war raised the debt by £277,000,000, but by it England was able to push her way in India, to secure the few possessions belonging to France which seemed worth taking, and, at the same time, without interference, to make for herself the outline of a new Colonial Empire in the southern hemisphere.

The second part of the French wars secured for us Tobago, St. Lucia, and the Isle of France, generally called Mauritius, all of which were important sugar islands; while we took from the Dutch the Cape of Good Hope, Demerara, Essequibo, and Berbice.

When the Battle of Waterloo was fought, the outline of our present Colonial Empire may be said to have been fully drawn; and since then we have filled it in with wonderful rapidity. As early as 1788 we sent the first batch of convicts to Sydney, now the capital of New South Wales. In 1829 a Settlement was first made in Western Australia. In 1836 South Australia, with its capital Adelaide, was occupied; three years later New Zealand was first permanently colonised. In 1850 Victoria was made a separate Colony. Besides these additions to our Colonial Empire in the antipodes, we also made some additions of small places, partly for military purposes, partly for trade. In 1819 we took Singapore, and in 1839 Aden. In 1824 we captured Rangoon from the Burmese, and in 1841 Hong-Kong from the Chinese. Besides this, our Canadian Colonists spread till they joined hands with the British Columbians on the west, and the Hudson's Bay Company to the north.

In South Africa, the Dutch, disliking the English rule, have three times made new Settlements—in Natal, in the Orange Free States, and in the Transvaal. Natal we annexed permanently in 1844; the Orange Free States we annexed in 1848, and let them go again in 1853; the Transvaal we annexed in 1877, and restored to self-government in 1881.

In drawing this picture of the way by which we gained our Colonies, I have not tried to soften matters, or to gloss over conduct which may be thought to be immoral; but I have endeavoured to set before you things as they were, and we must now make an attempt to put these facts together. The great points to be noted are these—(1) That the great change which has been going on in the world for centuries is the gradual substitution of large States for small, so that now we reckon the power of States, not by their size relative to Europe, but by their size relative to the world. States of the size of the British Empire, the United States, and Russia will be the types of the future; and France and Germany are beginning to feel this, and to make frantic efforts to possess themselves of a Colonial Empire while there are still lands to spare. (2) That England has twice won a Colonial Empire, simply because our ancestors set clearly before themselves what they wanted to get, and always kept that object in view, which is the greatest cause of the success of the policy of any country. (3) That France, and Spain, and England have each lost a Colonial Empire; France, by embarrassing herself with European wars; Spain, by trying to bind young nations in the fetters of an old-world policy; England, because she was foolish enough, at a particular moment, to make her Colonies see that they had more to lose by staying with her than by leaving her.

These seem to me to be the chief lessons we can gather from the history of the past, and I shall resume the study of the problem of the present and the future in my next lecture.

LECTURE II.

WHAT OUR COLONIES ARE, AND WHY WE KEEP THEM.

THE first step towards appreciating the value of our English Colonies is to try and get some sort of notion of them as a whole; and, second, to group them together, so as to form some idea of the way in which they are connected with the mother country. Our present Colonies, excluding India, may be arranged under four heads.

The first of these includes:—

1. The North American Colonies, of which the chief is Canada.

2. The West Indies, of which Jamaica is a type.

3. The South African Colonies, of which the Cape of Good Hope is the most important.

4. The Australian Colonies, in company with which we generally think of New Zealand.

These are all Colonies to which emigration is more or less desirable.

Next come a group of trading stations, scattered all over the world, often in very unhealthy places, where merchants settle for a time for purposes of trade. Such are Lagos on the west coast of Africa, and Hong-Kong in China.

Thirdly, we have a class of possessions which are neither Colonies for emigration nor Settlements for trade. Our Colonies are like portions of a great army stationed many miles from one another; and it is, therefore, necessary to keep up their communications with the main body or mother country by means of a number of connecting links. Moreover, it is not thought well that ships should have to sail far without coming to some friendly port, where they could escape the pursuit of an enemy, repair the damages done by storm, or replenish their stock of coal. Such links are the Isle of St. Helena, off the coast of South Africa, which was of great importance to us when the Dutch had the Cape of Good Hope; and Mauritius, at the other side of Africa, in the Indian Ocean. Then, on the road to India, we hold Gibraltar at the entrance of the Mediterranean, Malta, Cyprus, Aden at the mouth of the Red Sea (perhaps we may say Egypt), and the Island of Socotra. Beyond India, on the way to the Pacific, we hold Singapore; and on the other side of the world, near Cape Horn, we have the Falkland Islands, and a variety of other places of smaller importance in different parts of the ocean. You will see, then, that the importance of the first and second classes depend upon their intrinsic value; but the importance of the connecting links depends upon their position, and cannot be at all estimated by an examination of the chances they give for emigration or opportunities for trade.

We will now try to place before ourselves the size

of the British dominions. If I say that they amount to eight million square miles, I suppose it will give very little idea, so we must try and work by comparison. If one looks at the map of Europe and Asia, one is at once struck by the enormous extent of the territories which are possessed by the Emperor of Russia. Yet if one includes British India in our calculation, then the size of the dominions of the Queen, scattered throughout the world, exceeds that of Russia by about an eighth! That is one way of looking at it. Again, another place one thinks of as very large is the United States. The United States is slightly more than one-third of the size of the British Empire! No other European State comes anywhere near these dimensions; France, with all her possessions, is only the sixteenth part of this; Germany, which has practically no Colonial possessions, the fortieth.

Now let us look at it from another point of view. For every square mile of her own area England has sixty-five square miles of Colony; while France has not quite two. So that it would be possible to take an area equal to that of England and lay it down sixty-five times in our Colonial possessions; or, in other words, we have one England at home and sixty-five abroad. So much for the size; now for its population.

At the present time Canada contains four million and a half souls—that is, twice as many Englishmen as live in the West Riding; the West Indian Islands one and a half million—that is, as many as live in Northumberland, Cumberland, and Durham; South Africa one and three-quarter million, of whom not half are English—that is, as many as live in Northumberland, Cumberland, Durham, and Westmoreland; while Australia has three millions, rather less than the inhabitants of Lancashire, and rather more than those of Yorkshire; that is to say, in our Colonies live very nearly eleven million persons—more than a third of the population of England, Wales, and Scotland. Another way of looking at it, is to say that Canada and the West Indies have more inhabitants than Ireland; and that Australia has not very far off as many inhabitants as Scotland.

These are large figures, but they show, not that the Colonies are filled up, but that there is still abundance of room. If Canada were populated as thickly as Great Britain, it would hold a thousand million people—that is, the population of England, Scotland, and Wales more than thirty times over. So that if the population of England were to double itself every thirty years, it would take about one hundred and fifty years to fill Canada alone. I hope this will give some idea of how large our Colonies are, and what a vast field they offer for the reception and employment of our surplus population for ages to come.

I daresay you will now have had enough of statistics; so I will turn to another subject. Supposing that the whole world, except our Colonies, were closed to English ships, there is no product of nature which could not be provided by one or other of them, or any article of manufacture which it would be out of the power of one or other of them to learn to make, if it were worth their while. Canada has an enormous area capable of growing corn ; the West Indies can supply us with sugar, coffee, and tobacco ; Australia with wool and meat ; Assam and India with rice and tea ; Canada with timber ; New Zealand with hides and meat.

It hardly enters into the scope of these lectures to give a detailed account of the resources of each of the Colonies, and the opportunities they offer for emigration, because I am addressing you, not as intending Colonists, but as Englishmen ; and so I am trying to look at the Colonies as a whole, and not at each of them individually.

I may, however, remind you that the greater part of our Colonies are self-governing. The Dominion of Canada, the Colonies of South Africa, and those of Australia and New Zealand have each a Government modelled on the constitution of England. In each, the governor, appointed by England, stands in the place of the Sovereign, and is the honorary head of the Government. Each has a Parliament, consisting sometimes of one, sometimes of two houses, elected by the people. The Ministry is chosen, as ours is, from that party which has a majority in the lower house of the Legislature. The Colonies have thus complete control over their laws, their expenditure, their officials, and their soldiers. Each provides for its own defence, having a militia, and usually a few vessels of war for the defence of the coast. Each has its special difficulty—Canada, its French population and its Indian subjects; South Africa, its Dutch and native population:—but these matters they manage for themselves; only in questions which affect the whole Empire are they under the control of the Home Government. The West Indian islands and our smaller Colonies and stations are practically ruled by the governor and a small council, and, as a rule, have no Parliaments. In the case of the West Indies, this is due to the fact that the vast majority of the population is negro, and in other stations either the same is the case, or it is thought better to put the whole government into the hands of the military governor, as is done at Gibraltar. With these small exceptions, however, the Colonies are as self-governing as the mother country.

We will now turn to the special question of this lecture—Why are our Colonies worth preserving? To answer this, it will be best to examine what has been thought of Colonies by other nations, for what reasons they have preserved them, and to see what lessons we may learn from their experience.

There are a variety of ways of looking at the relations between Colonies and the mother country. Some have compared them to the fruit of a tree, which is thrown off by the parent in its strength, falls when ripe, and if it chances to light upon good ground, itself becomes a new tree, destined in turn to throw off new saplings. Others regard the Colonies in the light of children, which in their infancy are watched over, protected, and trained by the mother; but as they advance in years gradually learn to walk alone, and in time even, if they do not quarrel among themselves, are at any rate connected only by a very slight tie of mutual regard.

Now, I do not think that either of these comparisons is perfectly suited to explain the relations of a mother country and her Colonies at the present time. The analogy of the tree assumes that the parent stock is, at any rate for a long time, capable of producing, year after year, fruit of the same kind as at first, each successive crop of which runs the same course as that which preceded it. That analogy might do very well so long as the surface of the globe was practically unlimited; but it is unsuitable to the present state of things, when we are certain, in a way that our forefathers never were, that almost all the surface of the globe, habitable by Europeans, has been appropriated either by them or their Colonies or by nations like the Chinese, which are just as tenacious of their rights as we are. We may therefore assume that the crop of Colonies England has now is her last crop, and that if we lose these we shall not have the opportunity of re-creating a new Colonial Empire as we did when George III. and his friends lost us the United States.

We must therefore fall back upon the analogy of a family, and see whether that will offer any truer explanation of the relationship. There is no doubt that in the past this analogy has in the main held good. Till quite modern times all nations have been in the habit of keeping their Colonies in leading-strings. As time has gone on, these restrictions have been resented, and the Colonies have shown their resentment by separating themselves from the mother country. Such is the history of the United States, and of Chili and Peru. But I should like to point out that we in England in our treatment of our Colonies since the American War of Independence have pursued a different plan. Only for a very short time did we try the old leading-string principles. One by one our great Colonies in North America, South Africa, and the Antipodes have been made self-governing and self-defending, and so as we have begun by treating our children as grown up, there will not be necessarily the natural impatience which a boy feels when he gets too old for the schoolroom, and wishes to go out into the world.

Now, the feeling which exists between the grown-up members of the same family towards the heads of the family and towards one another depends very much indeed upon fashion; I mean by this that if most families hold closely together, it is much more serious for any family which breaks up, because the members of it have then to compete as individuals, not against other individuals, but against family groups; and, consequently, if one family holds together, a pressure is brought upon all other families to do the same. In the same way, if one nation and its offshoots unite together, it makes it more serious for any other nation to allow itself to be broken up. You will see, then, that the old analogy of the tree and its fruit is out of date, because there is no room now for the throwing off of new Colonies; and, similarly, the analogy of the family is inapplicable, because we in England have ceased to treat our Colonies as children.

There is also another reason. In old days it was assumed that a State could not be very large; but our ideas have changed. We now see great States holding together, not merely under a despotic ruler like the Emperor of Russia, but under a free Government like the United States, and the United States have even fought a bloody war in order to prevent some of their members from splitting off from the rest. If, then, these two analogies must be thrown aside, and we need no longer expect Colonies, necessarily, either to fall off like the fruit of a tree, or to leave us like grown-up children sometimes do, it is clear that the sooner we free our minds from those two analogies the better, or we may be in danger of becoming the slaves of a false idea. We are now, therefore, in a position to argue about the value of our Colonies as an open question, and to see what can be said for their retention.

The problem before us differs a good deal from that which presented itself to our ancestors. The question for them was, "Is it worth while to make great sacrifices of men and money in order to get Colonies?"—and to this they answered "Yes." The question for us is, "Is it worth while to retain our

Colonies, and what steps should we take for this end?"

Though we have not to consider, like the French or Germans, the question whether it is worth while to begin the foundation of Colonies, it is obvious that to some extent at least the reasons which they have for founding Colonies hold good for our retaining them; and, therefore, it is worth our while to begin by inquiring, "What has induced nations to send out Colonies, and how far are these causes applicable to our own case?" And I will first mention those causes which have ceased to influence us.

First of these stands the foundation of Colonies as penal settlements. You will remember that New South Wales, Norfolk Island, and Tasmania were originally intended expressly as penal settlements; and indeed I believe that others of our Colonies, particularly the West Indies, have been supplied with labour from this source. We in England have now given up the practice of founding penal Colonies, or of transporting our convicts to those which already exist; but it is worth noticing that our neighbours the French still regard this object as of value, and use their islands in the Pacific for this purpose, which is one cause of the complaints which are made by the Australians of the making of French settlements in their neighbourhood.

The next object has been the foundation of Colonies by exiles, either for religious or political causes, to which we owe the foundation of Maryland by the Roman Catholics, and the New England States by the Puritans. This cause has practically ceased to operate, except in the case of Irishmen, who go, however, not to our Colonies, but to the United States.

The third object is the formation of military garrisons. This was the idea with which most of the Roman Colonies were founded, with a view either to maintaining Roman rule among a hostile population, or to the keeping up of a chain of links between the heart of the Empire and its extremities. At present we do not employ the first class, though we have a curious instance of it in Carlisle, which was repeopled by Hampshire peasants from the New Forest in order that they might hold the Border against the Scots. Of the second kind are Gibraltar and Aden, and their value clearly is conditional upon that of the Colonies or Dependencies to which they link us; and, therefore, if it is worth while to retain these, it is worth our while to keep the military posts upon which our communication with them depends.

A fourth use which has been made of Colonies in almost all times has been the collection from them of a direct revenue, either by way of tribute, which was collected by the ancient States, such as Athens and Persia, and in modern times by Spain and Portugal, or indirectly by commercial restrictions for the benefit of the mother country. To sum up, then, what we do not do with our Colonies:—We do *not* use them as penal stations; we do *not* collect tribute from them; we do *not* value them as outlets for our discontented population. How then are they of use to us? The answer to this must be given as follows:—

Our Colonies are of use to us—(1) Because they increase our trade. (2) Because they act as an outlet for our surplus population. (3) Because the union between the English who live in England and those who live in the Colonies gives us all a better position in the world than we should have as little independent States. I will now pass on to discuss these points in turn in the order here given.

I showed you, in my last lecture, that the great idea of the last century was that Colonies added to the market of the mother country; but I also pointed out that in those days Colonies were forced by law to trade only with the mother country, and as we do not make that rule now we must see whether we gain, commercially, by the connection.

In order to understand this, we must ask ourselves—(1) What is our present trade with the Colonies? (2) Is it greater or is it less than it was? (3) Is it likely to increase or to decrease? In answering these questions, I shall, of course, have to deal with figures, but I shall make them as simple as possible, so I hope you will be able to follow without difficulty.

In the first place, the population of the British Colonies, including India, is one-sixth of the population of the world; on the other hand, to our Colonies and India we send each year goods worth about £83,000,000; to the rest of the world we send goods worth £156,000,000. That is to say, that our own Empire does more than half as much business with us a year as all the rest of the world put together.

Again, setting aside India, our best foreign customers are the United States, France, Germany, Holland, and Belgium, through whom a great deal of our trade with Germany is done. In 1869, these five countries imported goods to the amount of £71,000,000, and in 1883 to the amount of £81,000,000; that is, in fourteen years their imports from England have increased by one-seventh. On the other hand, our four largest Colonies—Canada, the West Indies, South Africa, and Australia—took in 1869 goods worth £22,000,000; in 1883 goods worth £42,000,000; that is, in fourteen years their imports from England have increased by $\frac{10}{11}$; that is, they have nearly doubled. Therefore, in twenty-one more years, at the same rate of increase, the five foreign nations will be taking £98,000,000; but our four Colonies will be taking £99,000,000! Another question which arises is, whether our Colonies are taking more English goods in proportion to their whole imports than they were. I have made some calculations about that matter, and, so far as I am able to judge, the proportion seems to maintain itself, and, if anything, to show a slight increase—that is to say, if I am correct, the Colonists are showing a slightly greater preference for English goods over those of foreign countries than they were.

We will now look at the matter from another point of view. And I am indebted for these figures to Mr. John Marshall (of the firm of Marshall & Co.), the late Chairman of the Leeds Chamber of Commerce.

The population.	*Total consumption of British goods.*	*Consumption per head.*		
	£	£	s.	d.
France, 38 millions	17½ millions ...	0	9	3
Germany, 45 millions	19 millions ...	0	8	4
Holland & Belgium, 10 millions	18 millions ...	1	15	6
United States, 57 millions ...	27 millions ...	0	9	7
That is, generally speaking, about 10s. a head.				
Canada, 4½ millions	9 millions ...	2	0	0
West Indies, 1⅓ millions... ...	3½ millions ...	2	6	8
South Africa, 1½ millions ...	4½ millions ...	3	0	0
Australia, 3 millions	24 millions ...	8	0	0

That is to say that, as customers, two Australians are worth thirty-three subjects of the United States.

These figures are liable to be altered by two circumstances—(1) By the growth of Protection. (2) By a change in sentiment—that is, by fluctuations in feeling or fashion, such as that which makes people at one time prefer English to Geneva watches; or, again, American watches to English. With regard to the first, I should venture to remark as follows. I do not think we can reckon on any great change in this matter which is likely to make the European States or America less Protectionist than they are. Such a change may come—for instance, the farmers of the Western States may rebel against paying immense sums for protected American machinery, when they can get cheaper from Europe; but we must not reckon on such a change.

Again, the longer a country has gone on with Protection, the more difficult it is to give it up, because the interests that depend upon it have become more powerful than at first. On the other hand, if a nation has begun as Free-trading, and kept so for some time, it is less likely to become Protectionist, because the interests of those to whom Free-trade is an advantage have, in the same way, gained great solidity. Thus, in the time of Cobden, it was very hard to beat down the corn-laws; it would now be much harder to restore them. From this I argue that, while we have less reason to expect a change from Protection to Free-trade, we have at the same time less cause to dread a relapse from Free-trade to Protection.

Another remark I should venture to hazard is this: As countries get larger in area it becomes easier for them to be Protective, because within their own area they have a greater variety of resources than is the case in a small country. If we go far enough this is ridiculously obvious, because a small corn-growing State, where manufacturing was practically impossible, could never be Protectionist; while a State with facilities for both might think it worth while to be so. From this I should argue that, as the powerful States take a larger type, the position of small States, if the larger were Protectionist, would be almost unbearable, and, therefore, that there will be a constantly increasing pressure on Colonies to hold to the mother country, and not to set up for themselves.

With regard to the influence of sentiment on trade, it is to be noted that there is much truth in the old adage, that trade follows the flag, and that, as I pointed out, there is no evidence to show that the

Colonies care less for our goods compared with those of other countries than they did. Moreover, our position in England as the head of the Empire has the greatest influence in the matter. So long as we hold this position, the Colonists are sure to look to us. English fashions, English dress are certain to set the fashions with the English abroad, and if by any ill-management England ceased to be popular, we may depend upon it we should very soon feel in our pockets an alienation which might be simply the result of carelessness or of inattention.

I should conclude, therefore—(1) that the Colonies and India, in the aggregate, take more than one-third of the goods we manufacture for exportation; (2) that man for man they consume an amount out of all proportion to foreigners; (3) that their importance relatively to the rest of the world is increasing at a very great rate; (4) that if Protection is to be the rule in the large States of the future, the advantage to us and to the Colonies of trade within the British Empire is likely to be still further enhanced; and (5) that sentiment has much to do with the matter, and therefore the conduct not only of the English Government, but of the English people, both to the Colonies as a whole and to the Colonists as individuals, is of the greatest possible moment.

We now come to look at the second advantage of Colonies—namely, the provision of an outlet for the surplus population of the mother country. Now, although Mr. George tells us that, if only farmers paid their rent to the Government, we should be able to increase and multiply, so long as there was standing room, without any difficulty about feeding ourselves, I think this question of surplus population is likely to be a very important one.

The population of these islands is now 35,000,000, and as it seems to have the power of doubling itself every thirty years, and moreover, when we know that the pauper population is one and a half million, and when we read of able-bodied men in London and our large towns able and willing to work but unable to find it, we have good reason for saying that the disposal of our superfluous numbers is one of the most pressing questions of the time.

To the ancients, and indeed till one hundred years ago, there could be no doubt that Colonies were needed as outlets for population, because men, except under great pressure, were averse to settling in a foreign land, where the laws, the religion, and even the speech were changed, and where the settler was likely to be all his life an alien in a far country. On this point, however, the existence of the United States, identical with us in language and similar in government, has made a great change, and the United States are at the present day the rivals of our Colonies in competing for our emigrants.

Now, if we only looked on the surface of the matter, we might readily think that it is of no consequence to us where an emigrant goes, so long as he goes away. By leaving us, he leaves vacant a place in the labour market. Into this some one steps who was out of work, and we are thus relieved of the danger of the latter becoming a pauper. Now this is quite true, and even if it were all, it would be enough to make the emigration question important; but it is only about half the matter. An emigrant does not cease to have to do with us when he leaves our shores. While he is with us he is a *maker;* he now becomes a *purchaser.* Not only does A by emigrating leave his place for B, but with his new earnings he sends orders home for English work, which does something towards giving employment to C. This is the case wherever he goes, so long as his new country does not Boycott English goods; but observe, in the light of the figures I quoted above, of what vital interest it is to us at home where he goes. Take X, Y, Z, colonists sailing from England. X is bound for the United States; he will send orders to England for goods worth 10s. a year. Y is going to Canada; he will order to the value of £2. While Z, whose destination is Australia, will send for £8 worth of English manufactures yearly. This is quite enough to show how important it is that our emigrants should go not to the United States, but to our own Colonies, and it is easy to make out the sum gained by diverting an intending emigrant from one to the other.

To sum up, then, we see that our Colonies will afford us for years a splendid outlet, and, moreover, that as things stand at present, it is of the greatest importance to our commerce to maintain the popularity of our Colonies compared with the United States as fields of emigration.

Lastly, we come to the third point—the importance of our Colonies as affecting our political position. I pointed out to you that history shows us a gradual substitution of large States for small, so that we now compare States by estimating their size in the world, and not merely in Europe, and I ventured to foretell that States of the size of the British Empire, of Russia, and of the United States would be the types of the future. I also showed that, in view of the probable Protectionist leanings of these large States, such as Russia and America, the position of small States would gradually become more and more intolerable as they and their commerce would be more and more at the mercy of their overgrown neighbours.

But it may be answered, England did very well in Elizabeth's time as a small State; why should it not do so again? To this I would say: Our ancestors did not think we did so very well, and made every effort to increase the size of the Empire. Moreover, small States, it has been said, are like little boys—very happy among themselves, but very liable to be ill-used among big fellows; and it is a question for each member of the British Empire, whether it will throw in its lot with the others and try and hold together as the United States do, or whether it will take its chance as an independent State, liable to be bullied either in politics or trade, as little boys are by big boys?

But I may be answered: It is very well for the Colonies to wish to hold to us. We offer them Free-trade, we protect them with our navy, we fight in their interests, but they do nothing directly for us in return ; and, on the other hand, are constantly involving us in difficulties, which sometimes end in wars. Other countries had as great commercial advantages as we had, yet they not only paid less for defending their Colonies, but also they exacted help from them in men and money.

Now till lately there was much in this. On us lay the defence of the Empire, and except that they maintained a force of militia and a few ships for their own special defence, the Colonies did nothing for us at all. But all this has been changed. Without being asked, our Colonies, in a most generous manner, to which it would be difficult to find any historical parallel, have come forward with noble offers to assist the mother country in a war, with which, except as members of our common Empire, they have very little to do. One of these offers has been accepted ; and Englishmen of New South Wales have been fighting shoulder to shoulder with Englishmen from home by the shores of the Red Sea.

The importance of this event seems to me hardly capable of exaggeration. It is a spontaneous offer of help, not merely the ordering of troops from one country to another ; and I believe that the way the news has been received in this country shows that the people, at any rate, rightly value the significance of the movement. Henceforward, any one who attacks us will, when we are fighting in a good cause, have to reckon, not with a little island in North-

Western Europe, but with a State which comprises in its borders one-sixth of the population of the globe.

Lastly, may I ask you for yourselves to picture what the result of the loss of our Colonies might mean? Supposing it true that our Colonies trade with us more because they are Colonies than they would if alien States, their loss would mean the decay of our trade. "Decay of trade;" I cannot use an expression which calls up a more horrible idea—mills stopped, poor rates going up, discontent and misery rife and remediless. It is an awful thought, and surely to avert it is well worth the most earnest attention that we can give.

I have now briefly put before you a summary of what our Colonies are, and why we keep them. Perhaps you will allow me to add one or two remarks on, "How we are to keep them." I have no faith myself in schemes of political union which are unsupported by national regard. The British Empire is now one, and the question is not how to make it united, but how to keep it so. That, I venture to think, depends mainly on the attitude of the English people. The Colonies have been useful to us in the past, are useful in the present, and are likely to be still more useful in the future. Let us treat them as we should a friend of whom we could say the same; let us look with the greatest jealousy on anything being done to irritate their feelings; let us make it plain that their interests are ours; let us welcome with enthusiasm their manifestations of regard; let us be careful to show appreciation of offers of assistance, with an eye to the future, even if they are not absolutely necessary at the moment; and let us feel assured that, so long as we do this, we need have no fear that in the future the Colonies will take the first step towards a severance from the mother country.

LECTURE III.

WHAT INDIA WAS, AND HOW WE GAINED THE CHIEF POWER THERE.

IF you were to be suddenly told that the inhabitants of two little islands had taken upon themselves to govern a continent whose area was eleven times as great as their own land, whose population was seven times as great as theirs, and if it was added that they only maintained in that continent, including the army, one man in two thousand of the population, you would be astonished at their audacity. If you were also informed that the climate of the continent was such that the islanders could not possibly live there without the assistance of the natives, so that a simple strike on the part of all native servants would be sufficient to render their living there impossible, you would be still more surprised. And, perhaps, if you were informed that the islanders regarded this feat as a matter of course, and took very little interest in the affairs of the continent, your wonder would be even greater still.

Yet the facts I have told you are literally true. The Islands are Great Britain and Ireland, we ourselves are the islanders; India is the Continent; its area is eleven times that of the British Isles, its inhabitants outnumber us by seven to one, and, even including the army, we only maintain there one Englishman for two thousand of the native population. Is not this a wonderful state of things, and is it not well worth our while, as Englishmen, to try and find how and why we succeeded in gaining a position to which no parallel can be discovered in the past history of the world?

What, then, do we mean by India? India is the name of a peninsula which juts in the shape of a pear from the south coast of the Continent of Asia. On the two sides which come to a point it is bounded by the sea; but at its broad end it is bounded by an immense range of mountains, which sweep in a curve from east to west, and form a sort of wall to cut off India from the rest of the Continent. Nature has divided India into three divisions. From the Himalayas flow two great rivers, the Indus and the Ganges, the one into the Bay of Bengal, the other into the Indian Ocean; and the lands watered by these rivers and their tributaries form two of these. The third is the triangular district two of whose sides are washed by the sea, and the base is formed by drawing a line from a little south of the mouth of the Indus to the opposite coast. These three districts correspond nearly to the Punjab or basin of the Indus, Bengal or the basin of the Ganges, and the Deccan or southern India. The most important city of India is Delhi, on the Ganges, about equi-distant from the mouth of the Ganges and the mouth of the Indus.

If you bear these three districts and the position of Delhi in mind, you will have no difficulty in following what I have to say of Indian history.

Let us now try and form some idea of the size of India. Everything in Asia is on a vaster scale than in Europe. The Himalayas are about twice as high as the Alps, the rivers are larger and broader, the plains are greater; and so, though in the map India looks a small place compared with the rest of Asia, it is really a very large place when compared with Europe. In reality, if you take Russia away from Europe, India is about the same size as what is left; so that we may think of it as greater than the area we should get by adding together Great Britain and Ireland, France, Germany, Spain, Austria, and Turkey—that is, all the great powers of Europe, to say nothing of a few unconsidered trifles, such as Greece, Switzerland, Portugal, Norway, and Sweden. When, then, we speak of governing India, we must think of governing Europe, always, of course, leaving out Russia.

Now, although India is very like Europe in size, it is very different from it in other respects. Europe is divided into a number of countries, such as France, Germany, and Spain. In each of these all the inhabitants speak the same language, have the same manners and customs, and to a great extent the same religion. Every inhabitant of Germany or France loves his country, is ready to fight for it if need be, and would never think for a moment of helping Russians or Spaniards to invade it.

In India, we have nothing of the kind. If we want to get an idea of the state of India, we must take a very homely illustration. Let us suppose that the Continent of Europe were suddenly to receive a severe shake, so that all nations, peoples, and languages, were to be inextricably mixed up, some thicker in one part and some in another, but never wholly apart. And then imagine that things settled down in that condition, then we should have a very fair idea of the condition of India. There you find Hindoos, Mohammedans, Buddhists, Sikhs, Christians, Parsees, and worshippers of the sun and moon, living side by side. You find not less varieties of language than in Europe, but more, only spoken in the same streets. You find race-hatreds as violent as between Frenchmen and Germans, only between people who are meeting one another every hour of the day. Even the Hindoos, the largest of the native races, are not united. They are split up into castes, by which certain occupations are hereditary. The members of the castes hate and despise one another. A member of a superior caste, such as a priest, or a soldier, will consider himself polluted if he touch a vessel out of which one of an inferior caste has drunk. Between the Mohammedans, too, are religious differences as great as these, and it is impossible to point to any important section of the people of India who are united in blood, in language, and in religion.

You will naturally ask, How did this extraordinary state of things come about? I answer plainly. It is the result of conquest. It is due to the constant invasions from which India has suffered. These different races, languages, and religions are the result of conquered, and conquerors, and reconquerors being piled, as it were, one on the top of another. This leads us to ask further, why has India been so often invaded?

Compared with countries from which it is divided by the Himalayas, India is a very garden. The rich cultivated plains of the Indus and the Ganges form a wonderful contrast to the sterile tracts of the high table-lands which lie to the north and west of these mountains, and what wonder is it that in all ages the inhabitants of these uninviting steppes have always been eager to swarm through the passes of the Himalayas into the land flowing with milk and honey which lay stretched below? If the Russians were to-morrow to attempt an invasion of India, they would only be doing what the inhabitants of Central Asia have done many times before, and they would only be obeying the irresistible impulse which has always driven the inhabitants of the hills to try to make themselves rich at the expense of the men of the plain. Moreover, they would come by the same road.

It would be well for India if the wall of the Himalayas had no gate, but this is not the case. A glance at the map will show that one tributary of the Indus rises in Afghanistan, and flows through the mountain boundary by way of the Khyber Pass. The Khyber Pass is the gate through which the invaders have come times without number. On this tributary of the Indus is situated Cabul, the capital of Afghanistan, and a little further back lies Herat; so that any one who holds Herat has but one step to make to Cabul, and at Cabul he will be on the high road by which the invaders of India have passed into the plains below.

By this road conquerors after conquerors have passed in long succession, till the imagination in trying to follow them loses itself in the mists of antiquity. However, for our purposes, it will be enough to recognise three great invasions of India—those of the Hindoos, the Afghans, and the Mongols. The invasion of the Hindoos occurred at a time so far back that we have no written record of its events, but we know that the Hindoos came across the Himalayas from Central Asia, and that they drove the inhabitants of India to take refuge in the mountains and jungles, while they kept for themselves the fertile plains.

There they raised up a civilisation of their own. At a time when Europe was a barbarous country, India was in many ways as civilised as to-day. It had a philosophy of its own. It had poetry and art and architecture, and a highly organised state of society. But that happened which often happens; this cultivated nation became weak, and was unable to defend itself against the hordes of barbarians who were eager to swoop down from the mountains, just as the Hindoos had done before them. These invaders were the Afghans. Their attack was made about the time that William the Conqueror invaded

England. The Afghans were Mohammedans, and they hated the Hindoos just as much as if they had been Christians. Roused by the fanaticism of their religion, and allured by the hopes of plunder, the Afghans, under Mahmoud of Ghazni, rushed on the Hindoos just as the Mahdi's Arabs would fly upon the Egyptians at the present day. The contest was furious, but the Afghans won, and by degrees they set up Mohammedan kingdoms in India, and in most places reduced the Hindoos to servitude. This was the second invasion.

But the Afghans did not long hold their power in peace. About the time of Henry VIII., a new swarm of Mohammedans from Central Asia, called the Mongols, began to make their way through the mountains, and attacked the Afghans in the rear. The new invaders were stronger than the last comers, and in time they beat them, and made themselves masters of Delhi, and there they set up their leader as the Great Mogul. The first Mongol Emperors of India were very able men, and between the time of Henry VIII. and Queen Anne—that is, in the sixteenth and seventeenth centuries—they made themselves masters of the whole of India, beating both the old Hindoos and the Afghans, and united all India for a time under their sway. Since their days a few other invaders have settled in Northern India, but the Hindoos, the Afghans, and the Mongols are those which we must chiefly bear in mind.

Now, no sooner was India united under the Mongol Emperors of Delhi than it began to break up again. This was due to two causes—(1) Their rule was an hereditary despotism. In an hereditary despotism, especially in the East, where the temptations to lead an idle and luxurious life are very great, it is usually the case that the character of the sovereign deteriorates. The first is always a man of ability, for he cannot make himself a despot unless he is one. His son often has the same qualities, but the grandson or the great-grandson, born in a palace, waited on by slaves, accustomed to every luxury, is usually a spoilt child, and an incapable man. When he comes to rule the Empire, the central power, on which its union depends, grows weak. That is the first cause of decay. Secondly, the Empire is too large to be governed by one man. It is therefore necessary to delegate power to governors. Under the Great Mogul, the governor was called a Nabob or a Rajah. Now, as soon as the office of Mogul was held by one of the luxurious sovereigns I have described, the Nabobs and Rajahs began to set his power at defiance. They handed down their places to their sons, they did as they thought fit, and they made every effort to become independent sovereigns. Consequently, the Mogul grew weak while the Nabobs and Rajahs grew strong.

When this happened, some of the old Hindoo chieftains began to lift up their heads, and by siding first with the Nabobs and then with the Mogul, as suited them best, they gradually made themselves all but independent. The consequence of this state of decay was naturally disorder. Good government was impossible when the rulers were all fighting among themselves; so bands of robbers sprang up, men, like Robin Hood in England, who became so powerful that their leaders actually made themselves independent princes, and defied the power of Mogul and Nabob alike. The result of all this was that India was rapidly falling into a state of anarchy, trade was falling off, and the only people who were doing a good business were the bands of professional soldiers, who hired themselves out to fight on one side or the other.

There were certain people in India to whom this state of things was exceedingly serious. These were the European merchants, who, about the time of the first Mongol invasion, had found their way round the Cape of Good Hope, and settled in the towns on the coast for the purpose of trade. The first to come were the Portuguese, then the Dutch, then the English, and last the French. The Englishmen who came were members of the East India Company.

This Company, which was exactly like any railway company of the present day, was made up of a body of shareholders, who chose a number of directors to manage their affairs. The Company was formed in 1600, just before the death of Queen Elizabeth, and received a charter from the Government. The majority of the shareholders stayed in London, but they sent out agents, called factors, to trade with the natives, and when they acquired stations the head of each was called a governor. The first station where the Company established a factory was at Surat, in

1611; the next was at Madras, in 1639. Both these are in Southern India, one on the west the other on the east. The ground on which their warehouses were built was rented from the chief of the district, just as a German, setting up business in Leeds, would hire his premises from some landlord at the present day. The next station, an island named Bombay, was given to the English by the Portuguese in return for some help we gave them against the Spaniards. In 1696, the Company hired from the Nabob of Bengal a new settlement at Calcutta, near the mouth of the Ganges. These three settlements—Madras, Bombay, and Calcutta—are at the present time the centres of British rule in India. While the English Company was thus making settlements, the Portuguese, Dutch, and French, were doing the same.

Of course the state of anarchy into which India was falling in the beginning of the eighteenth century—that is, about the reigns of George I. and George II.—was fatal to trade. Hitherto, the European settlers had devoted themselves solely to trade, and had kept quite aloof from the quarrels which had been going on between the natives. They had no troops, and had had no wish except to be let alone. But now a change was made. You will remember how I showed you that, in those days, Frenchmen and Englishmen were constantly fighting for Colonies; and nothing was more natural than that it should occur to a Frenchman in India, that the present state of disorder offered to him an excellent chance of getting rid of the English traders, and gaining for his country a paramount power in India.

The man to whom this idea came was Dupleix, the Governor of Pondicherry, a French settlement a little south of Madras. He based his views on three discoveries. Being a man endowed with great penetration, he saw that in the constant quarrels which were going on between the native States, and particularly in the interminable struggles between rivals for the different thrones, any power which could sell its help first to one side and then to the other, would not only make a good profit at once by selling its help to the highest bidder, but also soon gain the superiority over them all. His ambition was to interfere in this way; but how could he make his help worth buying? How to do this was his second discovery.

He saw that, though personally brave, the natives had no knowledge of European discipline—that wonderful force which changes a body of men from an armed mob into a machine, banishes fear, and multiplies, as it were manifold, the power of civilisation over barbarism. Nothing like it had been seen in India, and Dupleix perceived that, with a disciplined body of troops at his command, he could do what he liked with the native princes. Then came his third discovery. He had in India no such body of disciplined Europeans, but he found that European drill-sergeants could impart this discipline to native soldiers, and make them, when led by European officers, almost as good as Europeans themselves.

These discoveries gave the talisman which opened the key to India. To get soldiers was not difficult. The professional soldiers, who had been accustomed to hire their services first to one prince and then to another, had no scruple whatever about hiring themselves to Europeans, for they had no national feeling, and a Mohammedan would just as soon fight against a Hindoo or a Mohammedan of another sect, as against an Englishman or a Frenchman, and when once he had tasted, as he said, the salt of his employer, it was a matter of honour to be faithful to the death. These hired troops were called then, as they are now, Sepoys. Armed with his disciplined troops, Dupleix began to interfere in the quarrels of the natives, and soon acquired for himself such influence that he saw a fair chance of realising his dream of conquest.

Now, when once the French had begun this game, the English had no choice but to follow suit. If they did not, they saw before them the certain prospect of losing all their trade, and perhaps being driven into the sea. So, simply in the interest of self-preservation, they followed the French example, hired and drilled Sepoys, and began to interfere in the quarrels of the natives, always, of course, taking the opposite side to the French. This naturally led to direct warfare between the French and English settlements, and while the English and French were fighting one another in Europe and America, the French and English settlers were fighting one another in India.

Sometimes one got the better, sometimes the other,

and Madras and Pondicherry were continually changing hands. Not only did the French attack our settlements themselves, but they stirred up the native princes to do the same, and for the English traders the fight soon became one for life or death. Happily for the English, Dupleix received no help from his own government. They could not appreciate his greatness; had they done so, a few of the French soldiers who were being uselessly slaughtered in Germany might have changed the history of the world. Instead of being helped, Dupleix was recalled, and no Frenchman of similar capacity took his place.

At this crisis the English traders were lucky enough to find among their own clerks a man of transcendent ability, a man of the highest military genius, and at the same time such a master of intrigue that he was able to match the natives with their own weapons. This was Robert Clive. This great man has a good claim to be regarded as the founder of our Indian Empire. He organised our Sepoys, he created a small European force, and he beat back the attack of the French and of the natives.

Two battles mark this stage of the conflict. The first is the battle of Plassey, fought in 1757, in which Clive himself, with a thousand Englishmen and three thousand Sepoys, beat at least twenty thousand men led by the Nabob of Bengal, who, under the influence of the French, had attacked and taken our settlement on the Ganges, and thrown the chief part of our Company's servants into the celebrated Black Hole of Calcutta. This battle showed that the English and their drilled Sepoys were more than a match for the huge, but undisciplined, armies of the Indian princes.

The second is the battle of Wandewash, fought in 1760. This battle was fought near Madras between an army of Englishmen and an army of Frenchmen. Clive was not there himself, but his troops were led by another great officer, Sir Eyre Coote, who stands only second to Clive in the annals of early Indian warfare. In that battle the English won, and some of their Sepoys who saw the action, thanked Coote afterwards for showing them what a battle between Europeans was like. This victory was of immense importance. Hitherto the natives had been accustomed to think the French better soldiers than the English, but the battle of Wandewash changed their minds. The victory of Plassey over the Nabob of Bengal, and that of Wandewash over the French, are well worth remembering as turning points in the history of India.

To beat the Nabob of Bengal and the French was not the only thing that Clive did; he first made the Company the rulers of a part of the territory of India. This he did by undertaking the government of the lands belonging to the Nabob. He did not depose him. The Nabob still enjoyed his title, his splendid palaces, his princely income; but he only reigned, he ceased to govern; and the English Company became the virtual rulers of a territory, of which Great Britain and Ireland only make up an area equal to four-fifths of its extent. To make his title thoroughly good, Clive for a sum of money obtained from the Mogul of Delhi a legal document sanctioning this arrangement.

Now, this arrangement of Clive's deserves well to be remembered, for it was the model on which all the additions to their territory which the Company made were based. The Company never destroyed a native government altogether; sometimes they set up a new ruler, sometimes they restored a family who had been expelled, but they never took territory from the natives and ruled it in their own name. They played a more modest part. They always acted as the agents of a native prince. That prince might not have a vestige of power, but he was always there to be looked at. Orders ran in his name, taxes were collected by his authority, but the orders really came from the Company, and the taxes, excepting the prince's revenue, were paid into the Company's exchequer. Of course the first interest of the traders was peace and order; and they soon began to take into their hands the native courts of justice, and to appoint magistrates who looked after the police and enforced the orders of the Company.

This change was at first by no means a good thing for the natives of Bengal. It was not likely that it should be. Their new rulers were simply a company of English business men, whose main object was to make money. The first thing they thought of was, of course, their *dividend*, and they insisted on their agents sending them home as much money as possible, and grudged every penny that was spent without profit. Moreover, the servants of the Company were poor men, their salaries were too often screwed down to the lowest possible point, and their only chance of increasing them was by taking bribes, or by trading on their own account. The result was that Bengal was governed on the principle of the father's advice to his son: "Get money, my boy, honestly if you can; but get money."

The natural result followed. The wretched natives were ground down under an iron yoke. Their sufferings were like those of the wretched Egyptians, forced to pay the exorbitant interest of the bond-holders, and their position was worse under the Company than it had been under their native rulers. If these went beyond a certain point they could be dethroned, but it was impossible to get rid of the Company. The consequence was that famine followed famine, and the Ganges was choked with the corpses of those who died of hunger and disease. Terrible stories of all this were brought back to England, slowly, it is true, but still they came, and the heart of the English people was roused.

Under the rule of the next great Indian governor Parliament took the matter in hand. This governor was Warren Hastings, who was made Governor of Bengal when the three presidencies of Madras, Bombay, and Bengal were united under one governor-general. Hastings was as able a man as Dupleix; and he carried out the plan which Dupleix had sketched, but had not been able to follow out. He fought against some princes, he intrigued against others, and he was uniformly successful. He defended Madras from Hyder Ali, a soldier adventurer, who had by his ability made himself Sultan of Mysore, and threatened to drive the English into the sea. He intrigued against the princes of Oude, and acquired from them vast sums of money with which he appeased the directors and paid for his wars against Hyder Ali. He even hired out the Company's soldiers to a native prince who wished to employ them in putting down his own subjects.

But when these things were known at home, a loud cry was raised against the Company's rule. The natives found a champion in the eloquent statesman Edmund Burke, and Hastings was impeached for his conduct. After a long trial he was acquitted, but his impeachment forms a turning point in Indian history as important as the battles of Plassey and Wandewash. Hitherto the Company's rule had been a curse to the natives, it now began to be a blessing. Hitherto the Company had been both traders and governors in one, but now Parliament insisted that government and trading should be divorced, and that one should not interfere with the other.

From this movement arose the Indian Civil Service, which is made up of the English judges, magistrates, tax-collectors, and other officials in India. These men had nothing to do with trade. They were well paid, and had no temptation to take bribes. They have numbered among them some of the noblest

Englishmen who have ever lived, men who, like General Gordon, loved the natives, and were willing to sacrifice their comfort, their health, even their lives, for the men whose welfare Providence had placed in their hands. Under the rule of these men everything was changed. Where Englishmen ruled order and good government, security, industry, and therefore prosperity, were to be found, and the English provinces began to present a wonderful contrast to the native states, where anarchy, misrule, robbery, and extortion reigned as heretofore.

In spite of this success, the Company's wars went on as before. No doubt you will wonder at this, and ask how it was that, now that the French had been beaten and the Company's settlements secured from attack, that the Company could not confine itself to quietly trading and to governing the countries of which they were the rulers. This was exactly what the shareholders were always asking at their annual meetings, and the directors always strictly charged each Governor-general when he went out to be sure and not be led into war, as his predecessors had been. Each Governor-general always promised to keep peace; but as soon as he arrived in India, he always found himself, sooner or later, engaged in war.

To explain why this was, I must ask you to allow me to use a very simple illustration. Supposing you lived in the end house of a row of houses—No. 1, say—and that a fire broke out in No. 9 or No. 10, it would not concern you much as long as the wind was not blowing your way. But supposing a fire broke out in No. 2, and you found that half the people who lived in it were fanning the flames, and half were trying to put them out. Suppose, too, that it was pretty certain that the flames would spread, and that you and your family could not do your ordinary work, for fear of what would happen, what would you do? Surely you would take the liberty of stepping in, and helping those who were quenching the fire to put down those who were fanning it. And you would most likely take care that the incendiaries should not again get the upper hand.

Now this is precisely what the East India Company did. Government in the Indian native States was so bad, that anarchy was the rule rather than the exception. Anarchy was fatal to trade, and put a stop to the Company doing any business outside its own territories. Nor was that all; the English were still in terror of the French. French emissaries were at every Court trying to stir up the natives against the English, and Napoleon, for one, never lost sight of the fact, that English power was vulnerable in India as well as in Europe or in the Colonies. The consequence was that no sooner had the English consolidated their rule in one province than they were forced to interfere in the next, either to put a stop to disorder, which threatened to spread to their own dominions, or to guard against French intrigue; and so, in spite of all the directors could say, in spite of the promises of Governor-generals, the Company were obliged to engage in war after war, and to undertake the government of territory after territory.

No sooner had they beaten Tippoo Sahib of Mysore, than they had to fight the Mahrattah chiefs. When the Mahrattahs had been subdued, and their territory brought into good order, we had to undertake the task of clearing the territory of the Mogul from robbers. When this was done we had to fight the Sikhs, who dwelt on the upper waters of the Indus, in the country called the Punjab, and the princes of Scinde, who dwelt near its mouth. In this way, step by step, we were forced to go on till we had subdued every State south of the Himalayas, and had either taken over the government of the native kingdoms or had forced them to become our tributaries and allies. It is impossible to go into the details, nor would you care to hear them; but in the year 1856 the great kingdom of Oude was brought under direct English rule, and from that moment the English Company became in fact, if not in name, the paramount power in India.

But you will naturally ask how was it that the English always won? It is not a sufficient answer that they were braver than the natives of India; for bravery will not do much for a man in a country where he must die if he cannot get native servants to perform for him offices, which in a hot climate must be done by them, such as cooking food, fetching and carrying, and manual labour. No; we must look deeper than this. Moreover, even our battles were not won by English troops. The Sepoys usually outnumbered the English soldiers by three to one, and sometimes by five to one, so that really, as far as numbers are concerned, it would be right to say that we beat the native princes mainly by the aid of the natives of India. Speaking generally, our success was due to two causes—(1) the weakness and disunion of the native princes; (2) to our employment of paid and disciplined Sepoys against the brave but ill-trained armies of the natives.

On the fall of the power of the Great Mogul, a struggle for existence took place—vassal princes, Hindoo powers, military adventurers, robber chieftains, all fought for power. In this contest for life, the English traders took part. As Darwin would have said, it was a struggle for the survival of the fittest, and the English traders showed that they were the most fit. But we must examine the matter further, and compare their chances with those of their rivals, and see what it was that made them so. In history, at any rate, every effect has a cause, and the cause here is not far to seek.

The first great advantage of the traders was that they were a Company. This is not at first very obvious, but let us look further. Mr. Seeley, in his "Expansion of England," explains this. In the first place, since the rivals of the Company were individual men, they could not hand down their ability to their successors. How often can you find a good general who has had a son of the same power? Moreover, at any moment he might be killed in battle, murdered by an assassin, or die of a fever.

Now, a Company never dies. It is always the same; it pursues its objects remorselessly, relentlessly, without faltering or looking back. It is sure to have the best military and political talent at its command, for, if it chooses, it can afford to pay for them. It is certain of good soldiers, for it can hire them at good wages; so long as it is successful, it can outbid any rival in this matter. These three advantages alone placed the East India Company on a level with its rivals. But they were not all. The East India Company had fortresses on the coast well supplied with munitions of war, and too strong to be besieged with success. Besides, the Company was an English company, and they had the power of England behind them. The English fleet secured their communication with England, while it prevented succour coming to the French. From the English Government they were able to hire English soldiers, and from the days of Clive some regiments of the regular army were always in the Company's pay.

Lastly, they were able to offer the native states advantages which could always secure for them the help of an English party. They offered the sword with one hand, but order and good government with the other, and hence they never had to fight a united people. In every state there was a party who preferred the English rule, and as there was no such thing as patriotism in India, there was nothing to prevent such a party from doing all they could to help to replace their rulers by the English. It was not merely to change their rulers, but it was to exchange a bad government for a good. If we put together these advantages, a long purse, a cool head, a powerful army, and a kingdom at their back, it ceases to be a miracle that the Company won; we may almost say that it would have shown gross mismanagement if they had not.

Win, however, they did, and in 1856 they had become the chief power in India. Hardly were they seated in this position when the Indian Mutiny shook their power to its foundations. We have seen how the fidelity of the Sepoy army was the keystone of the Company's success. For reasons which I need not go into now, the Sepoys mutinied, and for a few weeks our power trembled in the balance. What is important to notice is, not so much that we put the mutiny down, but how we did so. You have all heard of the valour of Havelock and the energy of Lord Lawrence; many of you remember the events themselves. But by itself even the valour of the English could never have put down the mutiny had it not been for other things; a body of men numbering one in two thousand can never by themselves keep down a continent.

The reason was this: we gained our power in India because of the disunion of the natives, we put down the mutiny by turning the natives against themselves. In the first place, the outbreak was strictly a military mutiny. It was not even a mutiny of the whole native army. The Sepoys of Bombay and Madras, with few exceptions, were true to their salt. Even among the Bengal Sepoys many remained faithful.

The movement never was an insurrection of the people of India. At the critical time of the siege of Delhi, in the march of Havelock, at the siege of Lucknow, native servants were as usual fetching and carrying, tending the wounded, doing the cooking, even when exposed to the fire of the mutineers, who might be supposed to be fighting for the freedom of India. Nor was this all. Our latest conquests, the Sikhs of the Punjab, were only too ready to fight the Bengalees, whom they hated much worse than the English; so were the little Ghoorkas from the hills, who had been such troublesome neighbours in times past. Many of the native princes sent us valuable aid, and by the united efforts of English soldiers, faithful natives, and friendly princes, this formidable mutiny was put down. The history of the mutiny showed in the clearest light that India was not united, and that it was still, as was said of Italy, not a nation, but only a geographical expression.

The mutiny, however, brought about a great change —the fall of the old East India Company. This body, which had had such a great history, and which had done so much in the past, was now dissolved, and its power was transferred to the English crown. It had long ceased to have the monopoly of the trade with India, and it was better for everybody that the name, as well as the function of government, should be united in one body.

Yet one step more. The efforts of the Company had united India more firmly than she had ever been since the time of the first Mongol Emperors. At the Indian Mutiny the line of these emperors, who had all along reigned at Delhi with something of their old splendour, though shorn of their power, perished, and for a time India was without even a nominal supreme ruler; but in 1876 this was altered, and the Queen of England, by assuming the title of Empress of India, expressed the fact that, as representative of the English people, she had now taken over the task which had dropped from the inert fingers of the old rulers of Delhi, and would henceforth govern with justice and firmness the two hundred and fifty millions of Asiatics who then became our fellow-subjects in India.

In conclusion, I may say that in the history of the English in India you may trace four epochs. First, that of Clive, which is marked by (1) the victory over the French, and (2) the first defeat of a native prince by a combined army of English and Sepoys; (3) the undertaking by the Company of the duty of governing the Province of Bengal in the name of a native ruler. Secondly, that by Warren Hastings, which is marked by the purification of the Company and the organisation of good government by English officials. Thirdly, the fall of the Company in 1858, and the assumption of direct responsibility by the English nation. And, lastly, the taking by the Queen of the title of Empress of India.

LECTURE IV.

WHAT INDIA IS, AND WHY WE STAY THERE.

IT is of the utmost importance for us at the present time fully to consider the question of our Indian Empire, because during the last year circumstances have occurred in the East which have deeply aroused interest on the subject; and I presume that all my readers are anxious to know what India is, and why it is worth our while to make such strenuous efforts, even to the risk of entering upon a European war, to maintain our power there.

I propose to try and discuss this question from a practical point of view. I do not suppose that you care so much about the glory of possessing a great Indian empire as you do about knowing what substantial advantages are to be found in its maintenance, and what disadvantages are likely to come home to you and your families from any catastrophe which might deprive us of it. India is too often talked about as if it did not concern working men and women, and I want to show you that that is a mistake, and that the working classes really have at least as great an interest in the retention of India as any other class of the community. I hope, moreover, to show you that that interest has increased, is increasing, and is likely to increase still further; and I hope you will therefore bear with me if I am obliged to quote to you a considerable number of figures for the purpose of bringing these facts home to us.

In the first place, then, let us try and make an attempt to realise the size of India and the number of people who live in it. India, as I pointed out to you, is the same size as all Europe, except Russia, but while that part of Europe contains only 240,000,000 of people, India contains 254,000,000, and, therefore, when we think of our trade with India we must think of trading with a population larger than that of all Europe, Russia excepted. This population is very unevenly distributed. Along the course of the river valleys it is dense in the extreme. For instance, Bengal is the same size as France, but its population exceeds that of France by 28,000,000; on the other hand, in each district there are tracts of mountain and desert which are almost uninhabited. Of this great population, by far the larger number are engaged in agriculture. Of its whole number, 80 per cent. are connected with the land, while in England only 8 per cent. are so. India, as a whole, must be thought of as a land almost wholly given to the production of raw materials. It is, therefore, the very opposite of England, which becomes year by year more industrial and commercial. The remainder of the inhabitants are merchants, traders, makers of dress, workers in metals and pottery, and a large number are professional beggars. This, then, is the population for which we are responsible, and we must now enquire how it is governed.

Our Indian possessions are divided under two heads, British Territory and Native States. As I showed you in my last lecture, the plan of the Company was to undertake the government of some provinces, keeping the sovereign as nominal ruler. In other cases they made treaties with the native sovereigns, who usually agreed to limit their army, to make no treaty with a foreign power, to receive at their Court a British resident, who gave his advice when called for, and sometimes to pay tribute. This plan has been followed by the English Government, and the Queen, in virtue of her title of Empress, is now head of all the Indian States, whether they are under her direct rule or not.

Of these native States there are now about 1,000, and altogether they pay £725,000 a year to the Indian Government, and have among them 381,000 soldiers. Of these, the most important State is that of the Nizam of Hyderabad, who has just offered a contingent of forces to the English Government. His territory contains 10,000,000 inhabitants—that is, more than Ireland and Scotland put together. The Rajah of Mysore, whose capital is Seringapatam, has 4,000,000 people, more than Scotland and eight others have over 1,000,000 each. These princes count their rank in accordance with the number of guns that are fired in their honour when they meet the Viceroy. They are guaranteed in their dominions, but they are expected to keep up a certain standard of good government, and cases have occurred of their deposition for breaking this rule. These States include 50,000,000 inhabitants—that is, more people than Germany—so that there are about 200,000,000 left who are under the direct rule of the Queen.

The Government of India is a very complicated matter, which has grown up out of the fusion of the Company's system with that of the English Constitution. I will try to make its essential points clear to my readers. According to the maxim of the English Constitution, the Queen exercises each of her powers through the medium of a Minister, who is directly responsible to Parliament. The Minister through whom she acts in Indian affairs is the Secretary of State for India. He is always a member of the Cabinet, so that he really represents the opinions of that body. The Secretary of State for India is assisted by a council of persons who are experienced in Indian affairs, who are appointed by the Crown, but the Secretary need not take their advice unless he likes.

The local representative of the Queen's authority in India is the Viceroy, and of late years he has always represented the views of the Ministry of the day. Though he is generally known by the name of Viceroy, this officer is more correctly the Governor-General of India, and his office dates back from the year 1774 when the three Presidencies of Bombay, Madras, and Bengal were united under the Governor of Bengal, with the title of Governor-General. The Viceroy is assisted by a permanent council of seven persons, appointed by the Secretary of State. One of these is always the Commander-in-Chief for India. Of the ordinary members, one is always a financier, and another is always a lawyer. In theory the Viceroy acts with the consent of his council, in practice he is allowed to override its opinion in case of necessity, that is, whenever he thinks fit. This council is called the Executive Council. For the purpose of making laws and regulations, the Viceroy adds to it a few other members, some of whom are always natives.

The Viceroy has the general supervision of the whole of India, but the country is divided into a number of local governments; of these the most important are Madras and Bombay, each of which has a governor and commander-in-chief, appointed directly by England, and has a certain amount of independence. Bengal has a lieutenant-governor, as have also the North-West Provinces and the Punjab. British Burmah and Assam are under the rule of chief commissioners. The territory of each of these is divided into districts, and a district is really the centre of Indian government; its chief officer is the collector-magistrate. This officer, who gets his name from the old days when his chief business was to collect the revenue, is the moving power in Indian government; his district varies very much in size, but may contain more than a million of people, for whom he and his subordinates are completely responsible.

To understand the functions of government in India, we must quite free ourselves from the ideas which we have in England. Here we expect government to do hardly anything for us, except to defend us from foreign attack, and to maintain the law-courts. All our local government starts from ourselves. In English towns we elect our town-councillors, who in their turn elect the mayor. The town councillors appoint committees of their own number to manage local affairs. They levy rates and they take in hand anything that requires to be done for the organisation of the town. In addition to the Corporation we elect our school boards, our boards of guardians, and thus indirectly a town like this has the management of its own affairs. When a county government Bill has been passed, the counties will do the same.

If we want anything done which does not come under the province of the Corporation, some enterprising people take it in hand and form a company to do it.

In India the very reverse is the case; nobody starts anything, everything has to be done by the Government, consequently the collector has to do for his district everything which is now done by the corporation in the town, and in the country by the magistrates, local boards, and the like. The work, therefore, of the collector is immense. In his capacity as collector of revenue, he must understand and be responsible for the taxation of his district, as a magistrate he is responsible for its order and well-being; he has also to play the part of stipendiary, decide all petty cases which come before him, and pass others on to a higher court. Besides this, he is expected to supply the governor of his province with information on every conceivable topic about which he may choose to inquire, and to supply him with the means of doing anything which he may wish to have done. In a few cases the towns have greater power of self-government than the country; but in general the Government of India is a benevolent despotism, of which everything for the people and nothing by the people is the unvarying rule.

So much for the internal administration. The maintenance of civil order is very easy. In India there is only one policeman for every 1,200 people, in England we are so disorderly as to require one for every 635. The judicial power is quite separate from the executive, and there is a regular series of courts, as in England, for the trial of civil and criminal cases, with an appeal to the chief court at Calcutta. Some of the judges are English and some are native, and the civil law administered is based partly on the customs of the country, partly on English law; while the criminal law is that of the celebrated code drawn up by the genius of Lord Macaulay. The defence of the country is in the hands of a mixed English and native force. The English number 60,000, or more, the natives are twice as numerous, and count up to over 120,000. There are, therefore, now two native soldiers to one Englishman. Before the Mutiny there were three to one, and, in the early days of the Company, sometimes as many as five to one.

The maintenance of so large a civil and military service is, of course, an expensive matter. But every penny of it is paid by India. The collection of taxes in India is a very simple matter. Except in Bengal, where there is a numerous class of large land-owners, who let the land to farmers as in England, the great mass of Indian land is owned by the Government, who collect from the proprietors a small rent in the shape of a land tax. This never amounts to a rack rent, but in the aggregate it is the mainstay of Indian finance. Besides this there is a tax on salt, which only amounts to sevenpence a head on the population, and the opium trade, with a few small customs duties and licenses, make up the remainder. There is absolutely no income tax, so that persons who do not own land, but are merchants or bond-holders, pay a ridiculously small sum to the Government.

The Indian Army has three dangers to guard against: (1) insurrection of the native States, with their united armies of 380,000 men; (2) an outbreak in British India itself; and (3) foreign invasion. The third is that of which there is most fear at present, as there is not much risk of the first two happening, unless assistance came from without. Our great enemy is Russia. The Russians must practically come through Afghanistan, either by Cabul and the Khyber Pass, or by Kandahar and Quetta. To enable us to concentrate our forces on either of these lines has been the object of the Indian Government; and the great railway lines of India are so arranged as to connect the frontier with Calcutta, Madras, and Bombay; and a line has also been made from Karachi, at the mouth of the Indus, to Peshawur, at the entrance of the Khyber, so that troops coming from England may land at the very nearest point, and hurry at once to the post of danger.

The success of our defence of India depends mainly on two points, the first of which is the attitude of Afghanistan. No Russian can get into India without passing through that country. He may be helped through, or he may have to fight his way through; and it is the main object of English policy that he should have to do the latter. If the Russians find the Afghans friends, it means that they would bring with them 100,000 warriors, the descendants of those who have twice before conquered India. If they enter Afghanistan as foes, it means that all those wild warriors would be on our side, and that any Russian army trying to get through the passes, would be forced to meet the English in front, while their flanks and rear were subjected to the merciless attack of the Afghan hordes. This is why the maintenance of a strong, friendly, and united Afghanistan is so important; and we may venture to congratulate ourselves that at the present moment the Afghans are our friends. The possession of India, therefore, forces upon us the defence of Afghanistan.

In the second place, we have to keep open our road to India. The central point of this is the Suez Canal. So long as we can sail safely to the Suez

Canal, the route to which is guarded by Gibraltar and Malta, through the Canal, down the Red Sea to Aden, and thence to Karachi, at the mouth of the Indus, we can send soldiers from England to the Indian frontier in three weeks, and that is a much shorter time than Russia needs to send reinforcements from Russia in Europe to the borders of Afghanistan. So long as the Suez Canal is safe and open, we have in this matter the better of Russia; but if we let the Suez Canal either fall into the hands of an enemy, or into ruin, as it soon would if, in a time of anarchy, it were not attended to, then we should be forced to send our men by the old route by the Cape, and Russia would be nearer the boundary than we.

I have now given you some account of the obligations which our possession of India imposes upon us. I have shown you the system of government which exists there. I have explained that its possession entails upon us the very serious responsibilities of providing for the integrity of the kingdom of Afghanistan, and of maintaining the freedom and efficiency of the Suez Canal. From these responsibilities the greater part of our difficulties with foreign nations arise, and I want you to put these plainly before you, because they constitute what we may call the debit side of the account. We must now turn our attention to the other side, and see what we gain in return.

We saw that we valued our Colonies, (1) as outlets for our population; (2) because they added to our power; (3) as markets for our goods. It is impossible to give the same answer in the case of India. India is not, and never can be, an outlet for our surplus population. It may provide some Englishmen with a career and a profession; but it is a place to which one goes in hope of coming back again, not a place where one makes one's home. The reason is plain. The climate is bad for European adults, and fatal to children. We may, therefore, put that ground aside altogether.

(2) Does India add to our strength? I do not think we can say that it does. It may be objected that the bringing of the Indian troops to Malta or to the Soudan proves the contrary. But we must remember that we can never denude India of English troops, whereas the Colonies defend themselves, and also give us help into the bargain. On the other hand, the existence of our Indian Empire constantly entails upon us great anxiety in the matter of foreign politics, and brings upon us difficulties with Russia, and Turkey, and Egypt, which we should not otherwise feel.

The advantage which we get from the possession of India is purely commercial, and in order to understand its importance it will be necessary to deal with a number of figures, which I will place before you as simply and plainly as possible.

Up to the year 1814, the trade with India was a monopoly of the East India Company. It was then exceedingly small, only as large as that done with Jersey or the Isle of Man, and it was thought that the habits of the natives were so unalterable that they never would become purchasers of European manufactured goods. In that year the trade was thrown open, and to the surprise of the world it reached in twenty years the value of £18,000,000, that is, nearly as great as our present trade with Canada. But that was only the beginning. In 1884 the total trade of India was valued at £154,000,000, that is, it had increased in fifty years eightfold. Now, we think that the growth of English commerce has been a wonderful thing, but it has taken England sixty years to make the same proportional increase that India has done in fifty!

Let us now turn to the value of our present Indian trade. The total exports of British produce from the United Kingdom are valued at £240,000,000 a year; the total value of our exports of British produce to India is £32,000,000, *i.e.*, more than one-eighth. This sum does not include £6,000,000 of treasure, and £3,000,000 of foreign produce, which gives employment to our shipping, though it does not give work to our manufacturers. £32,000,000, therefore, represents the amount of English goods for which we find a market in India. That is, it is worth £5,000,000 more to us than the United States, and a third again as much as Australia.

The most important articles of this trade are cotton, metals, machinery, railway plant, woollen goods, and coal. Of these, cotton is the most valuable. In 1882-83 our whole export of cotton from Lancashire was worth £76,000,000; of this India took £25,000,000, that is, India is worth as a customer to Lancashire half as much as all the rest of the world put together. Of the next importance is the metal trade, worth £6,000,000. This includes cutlery from Sheffield and Birmingham, and copper from Swansea. Next, machinery, and of this we sent £1,750,000, chiefly from Leeds, Manchester, and Glasgow. Next, railway plant, valued at £1,500,000, chiefly from Leeds, Middlesborough, Sheffield, Birmingham, Barrow, and Bristol. The trade in woollens is worth £1,250,000 to the West Riding of Yorkshire, and the coal trade £1,000,000.

These figures will show you how valuable our manufactures for India are, and how many towns are interested in them; in fact, the number of orders from India is one of the most important items in the prosperity of our great manufacturing towns.

Let us now turn to our imports from India. Of these the most important are cotton and grain. Last year India sent to England 10,000,000 cwt. of wheat, whereas ten years ago it sent about 1,000,000. In regard to the trade in wheat it is important to notice that its extent depends on the following circumstances: (1) abundant crops in India; (2) crops falling below the average in the United States and Europe; (3) low rates of freight; (4) low rates of exchange. The Blue Book just issued tells us: "When all these exist together the supply of Indian wheat which will be put on the consuming markets will astonish, as they have astonished, those who were but imperfectly acquainted with the capacity of India for the production of this grain." That is to say, that if any great calamity should befall the wheat crop in the United States, or if we and the States should go to war, the amount of wheat which India would be able to supply is immense. It is no exaggeration to say that so long as we hold India, and the Suez Canal is open, we need never fear dear bread.

Again, the last five years have not generally been years of brisk trade, and yet the amount of goods exported by us to India has enormously increased during that time. In five years our trade in cotton has increased by one-fourth, in railway plant by more than one-half, in woollen goods by one-third, while we have exported three times as much machinery, and nearly twice as many boots and shoes as ever before.

Having considered what our Indian trade has been and is at the present time, we must now see what is likely to be its future.

It is plain that what we are able to sell to India depends upon what the natives will buy of us, and, therefore, the future of our trade depends on the development of India. Now, India is deficient in three respects: (1) it is ill-cultivated; (2) it is badly watered; (3) it is deficient in communication. With regard to the first point, the cultivation of Indian soil is at present far behind that of the United Kingdom. For instance, the average yield of wheat in England is seventeen bushels an acre; in India it is only eleven bushels, and the reason of this is plain. No native ever uses manure, he is content to scratch up the ground with wooden ploughs of the most primitive description, and for other operations of farming machinery is practically unknown. If the cultivated area only of India was farmed as scientifically as English land, it could easily find food for 410,000,000 of people. No doubt a change will be made in this respect, and so soon as it begins it will be good news for the steam plough works and the manufacturers of agricultural implements.

But the lands which are at present under cultivation are only quite a small portion of those which are believed to be capable of tillage. In some provinces there is seven times as much good land lying waste as there is under the plough. Often the proportion is three to one, and some even of the magnificent alluvial land along the Indus is yet allowed to run to waste. The great cause of this is want of water. In England our farmers complain of too much, in India they complain of too little. In India there is very little rain, and consequently when the crops are growing, they have to depend for water upon irrigation.

To give you some idea as to the importance of this, I must ask you to think of Egypt. Egypt has always been celebrated for its fertility, and the magnificent crops which its soil is capable of producing. But the soil of Egypt extends exactly as far into the desert as the waters of the Nile are carried by means of irrigation. In Egypt this work has been carried on for ages, in India we may almost say that it is only beginning. To further illustrate the results, I may mention to you a circumstance mentioned by Col. Scott Moncrieff in the *Nineteenth Century* for February, 1885.

Twenty years ago a Frenchman built, twelve miles below Cairo, a weir intended to hold back the water at low Nile, so that it might flow over the land without pumping. Unfortunately, till last year, its sluices were left open, as the structure was reported unsound, so the farmers had either to pay immense sums for pumping, or to go without water and miss a crop. However, some English engineers from India, employed by Government, found that the weir was safer than had been thought, and by great care they closed the gates enough to keep up the water 7 feet 3 inches above its usual level at low Nile. For miles above the weir the fields were irrigated without the expense of pumping, and rich and poor alike secured their cotton crop through the good work of these engineers. The weir is called by the natives "The Bridge of Blessings." In India the great rivers of the Indus and the Ganges, besides many lesser streams, afford excellent opportunities of similar works, and the cheapening of agriculture and the bringing of new soil under cultivation is simply a question of capital and energy.

In the next place, India is much in want of means of communication. So large a country requires an immense length of railway system to open it up. Great Britain and Ireland have 18,000 miles of railway; India, with an area eleven times as great had, in 1884, only 11,000 miles. Now it is just in this matter of irrigation and railways that the Government is doing most useful work. You will recollect that I pointed out that in England railways and tramways and the like were always set on foot by private enterprise; while in India, if they were not done by Government, such things would never be done at all. To meet this need the Indian revenue is arranged so that there should always be a surplus over the expense of governing.

This surplus is expended in improving the country, and for this purpose the Government has spent since 1869, each year, £5,500,000. "Every year new roads are opened, and the railway system is extended; new schools, hospitals, barracks, and dispensaries are built, and the country is more and more protected against famine by increased irrigation." Besides this "it discharges all claims on account of guaranteed railway interest; it repairs and maintains all the *existing* roads, bridges, hospitals, dispensaries, schools, court-houses, and public offices; it keeps up all the costly barracks, fortifications, and military buildings; it works nearly 11,000 miles of railway; and it keeps in order all the innumerable irrigation works scattered over a country double the size of Great Britain and Ireland, France, Germany, and Italy all put together, at an average charge of £2,750,000. In other words, the Public Works Department has given the benefit of vastly improved means of communication, and all the requirements of civilised life and modern progress to a population of about 200,000,000 of people at a cost of 3½*d.* a head." (Indian Railways, p. 205.)

To show the effect of the railways in developing

the trade of India, I will quote some figures collected by the Bombay Chamber of Commerce: "In the year 1852–53, when railways were first opened, the imports of merchandise amounted to £10,070,861; in 1872–73, when 5,671 miles of railway were open, to £31,875,000; and in 1882–83, when 10,317 miles were open, to £52,098,670; and it must be borne in mind that these values do not by any means adequately represent the increase in quantities, as during the last thirty years prices have steadily declined." The Indian railways pay on the average 5 per cent. In regard to the irrigation works, the average dividend is 6 per cent., and, Mr. Cunningham tells us, "When the system is more complete it is certain that the returns will be still greater, and even now, in the North-West Provinces, the canals pay 8 per cent., and during the famine of 1878–9, crops to the value of fifteen or sixteen millions were saved from destruction by canals, a gain which actually paid in one year the cost of the canals that saved them." (H. S. Cunningham, p. 37.)

It is no wonder that the export of wheat and cotton is steadily growing, and it will grow still more in the future. India will be the more developed as a market for our manufactured produce, and as a storehouse of raw materials and grain, the further our perseverance carries us along the road we are now pursuing. The more the people of India make the more they will buy; the fact that the demand for boots and shoes has doubled in the last five years is a proof that European luxuries are coming within their reach.

We may also be quite sure that India will do its business with us and with our Colonies. At the present moment India is just as free to trade with one country as another, but the value of its imports from the United Kingdom and the Colonies is twelve times as great as those from all the rest of the world put together. Of the whole trade of India, the United Kingdom has 56 per cent., France only has 6 per cent., and Germany still less. Of the vessels that passed through the Suez Canal in 1882, 2,565 flew the English flag, and the rest of the world only supplied 635. This shows us who has most interest in the Suez Canal, and when we add that last year 87¾ per cent. of our traffic with India passed through the canal, and only 12¼ went by the Cape of Good Hope, it is clear, whoever else can look with indifference on the politics of Egypt, we, at any rate, cannot stand aside.

Now suppose for a moment that we were expelled from India or abandoned it. What would happen? Would things go on as they are? Certainly not. In the first case, a terrible blow to the purchasing power of India would be struck in the desperate struggle that would certainly ensue before we were defeated; and after we were gone, Russia would certainly endeavour, by hostile tariffs, to cut us and our Colonies out of all share in what trade might be left. In the second case, our abandonment of India would certainly be followed by an anarchy such as on a small scale followed the withdrawal of the Romans from Britain 1,400 years ago. In it all the work we have done for the material prosperity of the country would disappear; capital would fly before its attacks; and the commercial prosperity of India, built up with so much toil, would perish like a dream.

I need not picture to you the terrible results to England of such a catastrophe. We know something of bad times. No *bad times* that we have ever known would be even a shadow of what would ensue. Lancashire would be utterly ruined; Yorkshire would feel a terrible blow, and I hope you will agree with me that when we think of what value India is to us in the present, and what a mine of wealth it will be to our children and grandchildren, that any one who even for a moment suggests indifference to its fate, or stints his hand in doing what is needful for its maintenance, is trifling with the well-being, not only of his fellow-citizens, but of millions yet unborn.

But there is another side to the picture. Hitherto I have looked only upon the material importance of our connection with India; I must now ask you to look upon its moral side. To abandon or to lose India would not only be a blunder of the greatest magnitude, it would also be a stupendous crime.

It has been the pride of Englishmen that they have always regarded themselves as endowed with great responsibility in having alien races entrusted to their care. The deep sense of duty, which we believe to be a special heritage of the English nation, handed down to us from the days of our Puritan ancestors, has made us scorn the idea of holding rule over others solely for our own benefit. This feeling, I believe, has never been stronger than it is at the present day. Since the days of Edmund Burke, the feeling that sovereignty is a trust has been especially strong in the case of India. We have deliberately set aside the notion of holding that country for profit alone. We have set up before ourselves in Indian government an ideal to be reached, which may perhaps be called Utopian. But in practice it has steadily been our aim, without interfering with the cherished superstitions and prejudices of the natives, to offer to them all that is best of the riches of western civilisation. We have given them equality before the law, freedom of the press, and education; and we have brought within their reach all the material advantages which have been developed by the energy of Europeans. What, then, would history say of us, what could we think of ourselves, if we deliberately handed over the results of so much self-denial and forethought, this great monument of constructive genius of Englishmen, to the barbarous despotism of Russia on the one hand, or on the other allowed it to relapse into the seething chaos of anarchy, robbery, and crime, from which it has been rescued?

It would be a bold man, not to say an impudent one, who would ask any Englishman, even for the sake of a great and immediate gain, to commit the crime which I have here described to you; but when we see that in this case duty and interest point the same way, the question whether we should stay in India can admit of but one answer, and, if we make up our minds to stay, we must accept the consequences. We cannot, as I have shown you, keep India and at the same time do without a foreign policy. The very fact that we possess it gives us vital interest in Afghanistan, Egypt, and our route to India. Foreign affairs seen in this light become our affairs in foreign countries—affairs which are not the interest of any one party, of any one class, of the nobility, of the army, of capitalists, or even of working men exclusively, but of the whole English nation.

In conclusion, I should like to say one word. In the course of these lectures I have had to speak a great deal about war, and perhaps it has been new to some of you to learn what a great part fighting has played in building up the British Empire of the present day. Even now, frontier wars are not unfrequent, but I have no hesitation in saying that at no previous period of the world's history has so large a portion of this earth been preserved from the horrors of war as has been sheltered from it by the rule of the British Empire. How many of the 250,000,000 in India have ever seen a shot fired in anger? How long is it since England has been invaded? How often has there been fighting in Canada? Where can you find a record of war between Europeans in Australia or New Zealand? And when we compare the answers with what can be said of Spain, France, Germany, Italy, Austria, and Russia, you will see that in the past the preservation of peace has been one of the greatest functions which has been fulfilled by the British

Empire. Nor is it likely that this will be less in the future. The more closely our Colonies and dependencies are bound by common interest to the mother country, the greater will be the safeguard of the peace of the world. A great empire, with interests in every quarter of the globe, is not likely to go to war for a merely local or frivolous object. Little wars it may and must have, but we may hope that in time these will become rarer and rarer, and that we may find in the union of the British Empire, possibly in the practical alliance of the English-speaking race, the first step in the direction of the union of mankind and the federation of the world.

SUMMARY OF CONTENTS.

LECTURE I.

LECTURE II.

LECTURE III.

LECTURE IV.

Four Years of Irish History, 1845—1849. A Sequel to "Young Ireland." By SIR C. GAVAN DUFFY, K.C.M.G. Cloth, 21s.

Wood Magic: A Fable. By RICHARD JEFFERIES, Author of "The Gamekeeper at Home," &c. *Cheap Edition*, cloth, 6s.

A Police Code, and Manual of the Criminal Law. By C. E. HOWARD VINCENT. *Pocket Edition* (Abridged), 2s.

Krilof and His Fables. By W. R. S. RALSTON, M.A. *Third Edition, Enlarged*, 3s. 6d.

The Adventures and Discourses of Captain John Smith. By JOHN ASHTON. With Fac-similes of the Original Illustrations. Cloth or parchment, 5s.

Treasure Island. By R. L. STEVENSON. 304 pages. Crown 8vo, cloth, 5s.

Technology, Manuals of. Edited by Prof. AYRTON, F.R.S., and RICHARD WORMELL, D.Sc., M.A.

A Prospectus sent post free on application.

Universal History, Cassell's Illustrated. Vol. I., Early and Greek History; Vol. II., the Roman Period; Vol. III., the Middle Ages. With numerous high-class Engravings. Price 9s. each.

England, Cassell's History of. With about 2,000 Illustrations. Nine Vols., cloth, 9s. each; or in library binding, £4 10s.

United States, Cassell's History of the. With 600 Illustrations and Maps. 1,950 pages, extra crown 4to. Complete in Three Vols., cloth, £1 7s.; or in library binding, £1 10s.

The History of Protestantism. By the Rev. J. A. WYLIE, LL.D. With 600 Original Illustrations. Three Vols., 4to, cloth, £1 7s.; or in library binding, £1 10s.

Old and New London. A Narrative of its History, its People, and its Places. With 1,200 Illustrations. Complete in Six Vols., 9s. each; or in library binding, £3.

Greater London. Uniform with "Old and New London." Complete in Two Volumes. By EDWARD WALFORD. With about 200 Original Illustrations in each. Cloth gilt, 9s. each.

Our Own Country. An Illustrated Geographical and Historical Description of the Chief Places of Interest in Great Britain. Complete in 6 Vols., with upwards of 200 Illustrations in each. 7s. 6d. each.

Old and New Edinburgh, Cassell's. Complete in Three Volumes. With 600 Original Illustrations. Cloth, 9s. each.

Cassell's New Natural History. Edited by Prof. DUNCAN, M.B., F.R.S., assisted by Eminent Writers. With nearly 2,000 Illustrations. Complete in 6 Vols., 9s. each.

European Butterflies and Moths. By W. F. KIRBY. With 61 Coloured Plates. Demy 4to, cloth gilt, 35s.

The Book of the Horse. By the late S. SIDNEY. With Twenty-five Coloured Plates, and 100 Wood Engravings. *New and Revised Edition.* Demy 4to, cloth, 31s. 6d.; half-morocco, £2 2s.

The Illustrated Book of Poultry. By L. WRIGHT. With 50 Coloured Plates and numerous Wood Engravings. Demy 4to, cloth, 31s. 6d.; half-morocco, £2 2s.

The Illustrated Book of Pigeons. By R. FULTON. Edited by L. WRIGHT. With Fifty Coloured Plates and numerous Engravings. Demy 4to, cloth, 31s. 6d.; half-morocco, £2 2s.

The Book of Poultry. By LEWIS WRIGHT. *Popular Edition.* With Illustrations on Wood, including a Series of full-page Plates specially prepared for this Edition. 10s. 6d.

Canaries and Cage-Birds, The Illustrated Book of. With Fifty-six Coloured Plates and numerous Illustrations. Demy 4to, cloth, 35s.; half-morocco, £2 5s.

Dairy Farming. By Professor SHELDON, assisted by eminent Authorities. With Twenty-five Fac-simile Coloured Plates, and numerous Wood Engravings. Cloth, 31s. 6d.; half-morocco, £2 2s.

Dog, The Illustrated Book of the. By VERO SHAW, B.A. Cantab. With Twenty-eight Fac-simile Coloured Plates, drawn from Life expressly for the Work, and numerous Wood Engravings. Demy 4to, cloth bevelled, 35s.; half-morocco, 45s.

European Ferns: their Form, Habit, and Culture. By JAMES BRITTEN, F.L.S. With Thirty Fac-simile Coloured Plates, by D. BLAIR, F.L.S. Demy 4to, cloth gilt, gilt edges, 21s.

Familiar Wild Birds. By W. SWAYSLAND. FIRST SERIES. With Forty full-page exquisite Coloured Illustrations and numerous Original Wood Engravings. 12s. 6d.

Familiar Garden Flowers. FIRST, SECOND, and THIRD SERIES. By SHIRLEY HIBBERD. With Forty Full-page Coloured Plates by F. E. HULME, F.L.S., in each. 12s. 6d. each.

Familiar Wild Flowers. Complete in Five Series. By F. E. HULME, F.L.S., F.S.A. With Forty Coloured Plates and Descriptive Text in each. 12s. 6d. each.

Vignettes from Invisible Life. By JOHN BADCOCK. With numerous Illustrations specially executed for the Work. 3s. 6d.

The Magazine of Art. Yearly Volume. With about 500 Illustrations by the first Artists of the day, and beautifully-executed Etching, for Frontispiece. Cloth gilt, gilt edges, 16s.

Some Modern Artists. With highly-finished En-gravings of their most popular Masterpieces and Portraits. 12s. 6d.

The Forging of the Anchor. With 20 Illustrations specially executed for the Work, by the first Artists of the day. Small 4to, cloth, gilt edges, 5s., or Japanese morocco, padded (in box), 6s.

Picturesque Europe. *Popular Edition.* Vols. I., II., & III., with 13 exquisite Steel Plates, and about 200 Original Engravings in each by the best Artists. Cloth gilt, 18s. each; or Vols. I. & II. (containing the British Isles complete) bound in one, 31s. 6d. N.B.—The *Original Edition*, in Five magnificent Volumes, royal 4to size, can still be obtained, price £10 10s.

Egypt: Descriptive, Historical, and Picturesque. By Prof. G. EBERS. Translated by CLARA BELL, with Notes by SAMUEL BIRCH, LL.D., D.C.L., F.S.A. With Original magnificent Engravings. Cloth bevelled, gilt edges. Vol. I., £2 5s.; Vol. II., £2 12s. 6d., or the Two Vols. in box, £4 17s. 6d.

Picturesque America. Complete in Four Vols. with 12 exquisite Steel Plates and about 200 Original Wood Engravings in each. Royal 4to, £2 2s. each.

Landscape Painting in Oils, A Course of Lessons in. By A. F. GRACE, Turner Medallist, Royal Academy. With Nine Reproductions in Colour. Extra demy folio, cloth, gilt edges, 42s.

Illustrated British Ballads. With Several Hundred Original Illustrations. Complete in Two Vols. Cloth, 7s. 6d. each; cloth, gilt edges, 10s. 6d. each; morocco, Two Vols., 25s.

Sunlight and Shade. Original and Selected Poems. With exquisite Engravings by the best Artists of the day. 7s. 6d.

Choice Poems by H. W. LONGFELLOW. Illustrated from Paintings by his Son ERNEST W. LONGFELLOW. Small 4to, cloth, 6s.

The Doré Fine Art Volumes comprise—

	£ s. d.		£ s. d.
Milton's Paradise Lost	1 1 0	**Munchausen** . .	0 5 0
The Doré Bible . .	2 10 0	**Fairy Tales Told Again**	0 5 0
Don Quixote . . .	0 15 0		

The Book of Health. A Systematic Treatise upon Science and the Preservation of Health. With Contributions by eminent Medical Authorities. 21s. ; half-morocco, 25s.

Our Homes and How to make them Healthy. Edited by SHIRLEY FORSTER MURPHY, assisted by eminent Contributors. Royal 8vo, cloth, illustrated, 15s. ; half-morocco, 21s.

The Family Physician. A Modern Manual of Domestic Medicine. By PHYSICIANS and SURGEONS of the Principal London Hospitals. Royal 8vo, cloth, 21s. ; half-roxburgh, gilt top, 25s.

Medicine, Manuals for Students of.

Elements of Histology. By E. KLEIN, M.D., F.R.S. 6s.

Surgical Pathology. By A. J. PEPPER, M.B., M.S. 7s. 6d.

Physiological Physics. By J. MCGREGOR ROBERTSON. 7s. 6d.

Surgical Applied Anatomy. By F. TREVES, F.R.C.S. 7s. 6d.

Human Physiology. By HENRY POWER, F.R.C.S. 7s. 6d.

Clinical Chemistry. By CHAS. H. RALFE, M.D., F.R.C.P. 5s.

Materia Medica and Therapeutics. By J. MITCHELL BRUCE, M.D., F.R.C.P. 7s. 6d.

Prospectus will be sent post free on application.

Clinical Manuals for Practitioners and Students of Medicine. *A List sent post free on application.*

The Domestic Dictionary. An Encyclopædia for the Household. Illustrated throughout. 1,280 pages, royal 8vo. *Cheap Edition*, price 7s. 6d. ; half-roan, 9s.

Cassell's Dictionary of Cookery. The Largest, Cheapest, and Best Book of Cookery. With 9,000 Recipes, and numerous Illustrations. *Cheap Edition*, price 7s. 6d. ; half-roan, 9s.

Choice Dishes at Small Cost. Containing Practical Directions to Success in Cookery, and Original Recipes for Appetising and Economical Dishes. By A. G. PAYNE. 3s. 6d.

The Making of the Home. A Book of Domestic Economy for School and Home Use. By HENRIETTA O. (Mrs. S. A.) BARNETT. Cloth, 1s. 6d.

A Year's Cookery. Giving Dishes for Breakfast, Luncheon, and Dinner for Every Day in the Year, with Practical Instructions for their Preparation. By PHYLLIS BROWNE. 3s. 6d.

What Girls Can Do. A Book for Mothers and Daughters. By PHYLLIS BROWNE. *Cheap Edition.* 2s. 6d.

☞ **Cassell & Company's Complete Catalogue,** *containing a List of Several Hundred Volumes, including Bibles and Religious Works, Fine-Art Volumes, Children's Books, Dictionaries, Educational Works, Handbooks and Guides, History, Natural History, Household and Domestic Treatises, Science, Serials, Travels, &c. &c., sent post free on application.*

Cassell & Company, Limited: London, Paris, New York and Melbourne